The
Civilizational
Process

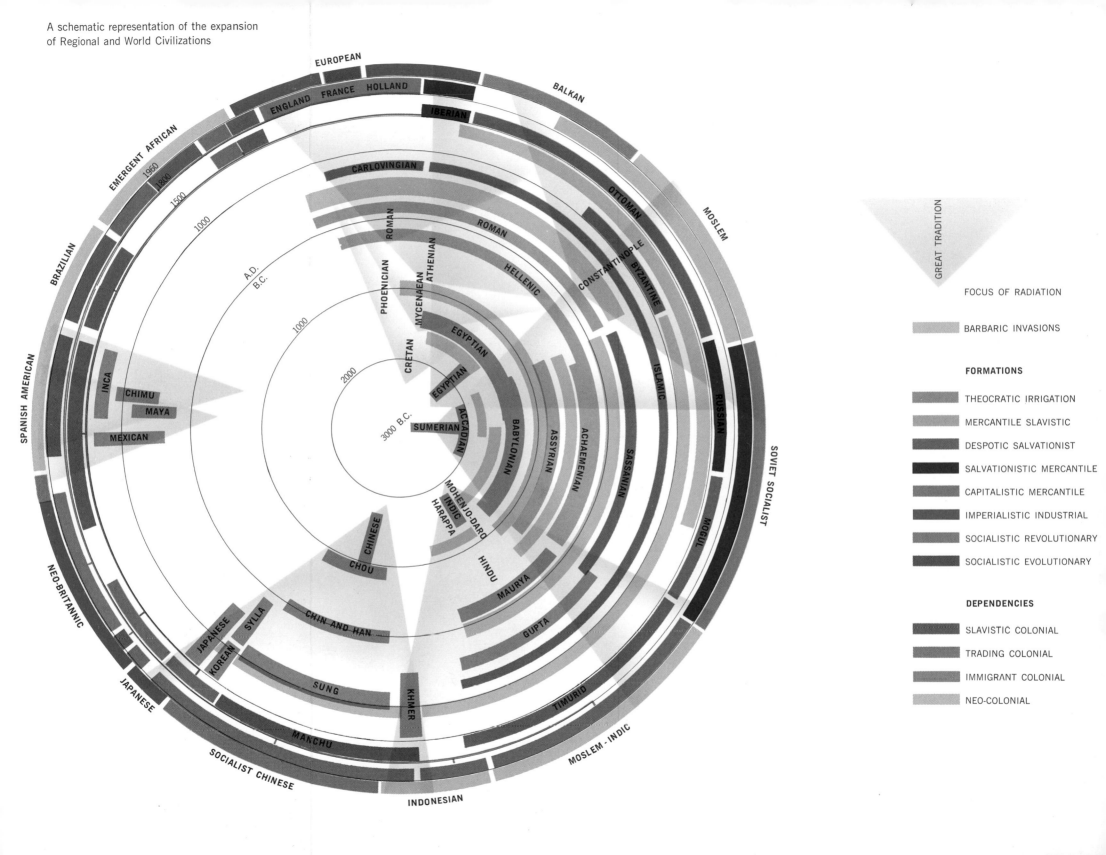

A schematic representation of the expansion
of Regional and World Civilizations

EUROPEAN

ENGLAND FRANCE HOLLAND

BALKAN

IBERIAN

EMERGENT AFRICAN

1960
1800
1500
1000

CARLOVINGIAN

OTTOMAN

MOSLEM

BRAZILIAN

A.D.
B.C.

ROMAN
PHOENICIAN
ROMAN
ATHENIAN
HELLENIC
MYCENAEAN
CONSTANTINOPLE BYZANTINE
1000
CRETAN
EGYPTIAN
ISLAMIC

SPANISH AMERICAN

INCA
CHIMU
MAYA
MEXICAN

2000

EGYPTIAN

RUSSIAN

3000 B.C.
SUMERIAN
ACCADIAN
BABYLONIAN
ASSYRIAN
ACHAEMENIAN
SASSANIAN
MOGUL

SOVIET SOCIALIST

MOHENJO-DARO
INDIC
HARAPPA

HINDU

MAURYA

NEO-BRITANNIC

CHINESE

CHOU

GUPTA

JAPANESE SYLLA
KOREAN
CHIN AND HAN

JAPANESE

SUNG

KHMER

TIMURID

MANCHU

SOCIALIST CHINESE

MOSLEM - INDIC

INDONESIAN

GREAT TRADITION

FOCUS OF RADIATION

BARBARIC INVASIONS

FORMATIONS

THEOCRATIC IRRIGATION

MERCANTILE SLAVISTIC

DESPOTIC SALVATIONIST

SALVATIONISTIC MERCANTILE

CAPITALISTIC MERCANTILE

IMPERIALISTIC INDUSTRIAL

SOCIALISTIC REVOLUTIONARY

SOCIALISTIC EVOLUTIONARY

DEPENDENCIES

SLAVISTIC COLONIAL

TRADING COLONIAL

IMMIGRANT COLONIAL

NEO-COLONIAL

THE CIVILIZATIONAL PROCESS

Darcy Ribeiro

Translated, and with a foreword by
Betty J. Meggers

SMITHSONIAN INSTITUTION PRESS
City of Washington   1968

Smithsonian Publication 4749
Distributed by Random House, Inc.
in the United States and Canada
Library of Congress Catalog 69–11052
Copyright © 1968 by Darcy Ribeiro
All rights reserved

Designed by Elizabeth Sur
Printed in the United States of America

Foreword

The subject matter of this volume is the most recent segment of human history, representing only a tenth part of *Homo sapiens'* duration on this earth, and less than a hundredth of the time since the first hominid started making tools. Yet even this fraction is equivalent to some ten thousand years, during most of which human beings lived under conditions far different from those confronting us today. Why bother to resurrect ancient history? Would it not be better to spend our time on more contemporary problems? In replying, let us consider a few facts.

The world today is in a state of upheaval. Wars, rebellions, coups, guerrilla activities, strikes, and other manifestations of unrest figure daily in the headlines of our newspapers. In the United States, we are faced with social problems of growing magnitude. "Ghetto" riots are becoming as inevitable as the hot days of summer, and they now threaten to destroy significant portions of our major cities. Racial conflicts express themselves in a variety of ways. Gross discrepancies in access to economic and educational advantages not only create special problems, but diffuse their disruptive effects throughout the social order. As if this were not enough, the average citizen is penalized for the unfavorable balance of payments that stem from policies of his government; or he is drafted to fight in a foreign war, the validity of which his leaders publicly debate. All but the youngest of us can recall "the good old days," when we seemed to have few serious problems, and life was comfortable, serene, predictable, and secure. What has made the difference?

One of the striking trends of recent years has been an intensification of rebellion, not only by the underprivileged, who often before in history have fought against their lot, but by the younger members of the middle and upper classes. The novelty of this behavior is such that new words, like "hippie" and "beatnik," must be invented to describe it; the behavior itself defies long-accepted norms of dress and conduct, creating severe conflicts between generations. Parents who struggled for education and financial security cannot communicate with offspring who drop out of school, find release in drugs, dress like the opposite sex, and refuse to fight for their country. "Alienation" from traditional values is a growing threat to the maintenance of social order. Why has it happened? What has gone wrong?

As if all of this were not enough, the human population is increasing at such a rapid rate that experts predict "standing room only" in a few more generations unless controls are instituted. Furthermore, man has long been remodeling the surface of the earth to his liking by damming and diverting rivers, leveling hills, obliterating forests, tunneling under land and water, and covering the ground with cement or asphalt. In so doing he has inadvertently been altering the delicate balance of nature, polluting the air and the water, modifying vegetation patterns, and setting in motion events that may ultimately make this planet unsuitable for human life. The conservationists warn of the impending doom, yet the commercial interests fight even harder for a chance to make profits. Where will all this lead?

The solution to any problem depends on an understanding of the factors involved. The existence of diametrically opposed opinions on how to deal with the issues confronting us today is the best indication of how little we understand the causes. Faced with the necessity of doing something, we resort to the traditional remedy: force. Since successful application of force achieves only a suppression of the symptoms, and does nothing to alter their causes, it can only postpone the day of reckoning. As the ineffectuality of police and military remedies for today's ills becomes increasingly evident, desperation grows. We feel trapped, imprisoned by forces over which we have no control, abandoned by the gods and sent hurtling to destruction. What is going to happen to us?

If understanding is the first step to rational action, then we must achieve understanding. The perspective provided by Darcy Ribeiro in this volume makes it clear that we are caught in the turbulence of one of the great cultural revolutions that have periodically traumatized mankind. Our technology has advanced more rapidly than the social and ideological sectors of our culture, creating strains that ultimately relieve themselves with the violence of an earthquake. The uncertainties, fears, and anguish; the rebellion, alienation, and frustration that we feel also must certainly have been felt by those caught in the midst of the Industrial Revolution, or the earlier Irrigation Revolution. Now, however, we have in our possession sophisticated techniques of scientific observation and data processing, and these place for the first time within our grasp the possibility of understanding what is going on.

On the other hand, we remain severely handicapped by our psychological involvement in the data we must analyze. What we have to dissect is culture, and culture is fully effective only when it guides human actions without human awareness. If we question our beliefs and the basis for our behavior, we run the risk of endangering our whole social order. This is why the hippies, the atheists, the homosexuals, and other kinds of nonconformists are viewed with suspicion and hostility: their deviation from community norms is a threat to social solidarity. In earlier centuries, such individuals were ostracized, burned at the stake, crucified, or thrown to the lions. In the larger societies of today, a few can be allowed to live, but they are branded as radicals or even subversives, and penalized socially in subtle ways.

Viewed from the cultural standpoint, however, these "radicals" are necessary. Social evolution could not occur without them. The perspective of ten thousand years makes it clear that numerous beliefs once "unthinkable" have subsequently achieved acceptance, although at the cost of much suffering. How many people were persecuted or even deprived of life for insisting that the world is round rather than flat? Or that the earth moves around the sun rather than vice-versa? Or that human destiny is not guided by the stars? Or that man has evolved from lower forms of life? Suppose that a scientific study of culture should reveal that some of the beliefs we cherish today are also false? What if it should be discovered that capitalism is not the ultimate form of social order, or that there are no gods, or that communism is not intrinsically evil? Fear of what we may discover impels us to turn away from too close scrutiny of our beliefs, but such scrutiny is essential if we are to reach an understanding of what is happening in the world today.

Social science, in its broadest sense, is modern society's institutionalized means of investigating the operation of culture. Because social scientists tread on potentially dangerous ground, however, pressures are applied to neutralize their effectiveness. As a result, sociologists have concerned themselves with "safe" subjects like social structure and have employed impersonal methods of investigation like questionnaires and statistics. Anthropologists have made it a professional credo that immersion in the cultures of primitive peoples is prerequisite to objective analysis of our own culture, and have seldom ventured onto the larger stage. On the other hand, economists and political scientists are more daring, but find more solid resistance to such proposed innovations as the guaranteed income, which challenge vested interests. A problem facing all these specialists is the common notion that, since everyone has lifelong, firsthand experience with the workings of society and culture, everyone qualifies as an expert. A political scientist is thus no more respected than a politician, an economist may be given less credence than a businessman, and a sociologist or anthropologist less than a military officer or a member of the cabinet—on the ground that the former are "theorists" whereas the latter have "practical" experience. Fortunately, there are signs that this view is beginning to change in the face of growing evidence that the advice of "practical" experts often does not work.

Of all social scientists, anthropologists have had the most to do with explaining culture. The history of this discipline has been characterized by violent disputes between the cultural evolutionists and the anti-evolutionists: between those who see culture as an entity to be studied in its own terms and obedient to its own laws, and those who see it as the free creation of man's intellect and responsive to his whims; or between those who feel that understanding of the past will permit prediction of the future, and those who consider the future unpredictable. At the present time, the evolutionists are gaining ground, and the view that cultural development results from the interplay of definable forces under specifiable conditions is achieving increasing acceptance.

The author of the present essay represents the evolutionist school of anthropology, and he presents us here with a new analysis of the "civilizational process." He brings unusual qualifications to the task. Born in 1922 in the Brazilian state of Minas Gerais, he was trained in anthropology, sociology, and political science at the Escola de Sociologia e Política in São Paulo. The first decade of his professional life was devoted principally to fieldwork among Indian tribes of the Amazon and central Brazil, among them the Kaduveo, Terena, Kaywá, Ofaié-Xavante, Bororo, Karajá, Urubú-Kaapor, Kaingang, Xokleng, and various Xingú groups. During this period he also conducted a two-year acculturation study under the auspices of the Division of Social Sciences of UNESCO, and organized the Museu do Indio in Rio de Janeiro. In 1956 he became Professor of Anthropology at the Universidade do Brasil in Rio de Janeiro, beginning an academic career that led to his appointment, in 1961, as the first Rector of the newly created Universidade de Brasília (which he largely planned). Between 1958 and 1961, while Chief of the Division of Social Research in the Ministry of Education, Ribeiro directed a program to investigate regional variation in Brazilian society and its significance for progress in urbanization, industrialization, and public education.

In 1962 Ribeiro began a third career by entering political life as Minister of Education and Culture of Brazil. During the next two years, he designed and put into effect the first five-year plan for the eradication of illiteracy, and the reorganization and democratization of the secondary school system, which also laid the foundation for reform of the university structure. He left this post to return to the Rectorship of the Universidade de Brasília, but was soon called upon by President João Goulart to head his "Casa Civil," an advisory body generally comparable to the Executive Office of the United States President. He served in this capacity until Goulart's overthrow on 31 March 1964, led to the exile of all those closely associated with that administration. Since then Ribeiro has resided in Montevideo, Uruguay, where he has resumed his academic career as Professor of Anthropology in the Facultad de Humanidades of the Universidad de la República Oriental del Uruguay.

This variety of experience has provided Darcy Ribeiro with unique opportunities to observe the operation of culture under the most diverse conditions: he has lived with tribes at the most primitive level and stood at the governmental vortex of one of the largest modern nations. He has studied and analyzed communities undergoing acculturation from the primitive to the modern state, or undergoing modernization from a rural to an industrial condition. Being a professional anthropologist, he has analyzed all these situations from a perspective different from that of the sociologist, economist, or political scientist. As a consequence, he has achieved novel and provocative insights into the operation of the civilizational process.

There is another reason that Ribeiro's work deserves careful consideration. We in the United States have inherited the mantle of western European civilization, which we look upon as the central or major current of cultural evolution. All other peoples are measured against us and most are found wanting. Our national political goals are based on the assumption that the direction of progress lies in making others more like us politically, socially, industrially, ideologically. The best known works on cultural evolution are the products of European or United States scholars, and as a result they explicitly or implicitly support this view. Ribeiro, however, is not a product of the Euro-American scholastic or political tradition, but a citizen of the "Third World." As such, he sees cultural development from a different perspective and consequently notices things that remain hidden to us. This is not to say that he has no bias simply because he does not share ours. Those points in his analysis that challenge our conceptions, however, cannot be dismissed on the ground of prejudice, not only because his professional qualifications entitle him to a respectful hearing, but because only by combining other perspectives with ours can we distinguish truth from distortion and so ultimately arrive at real understanding of the civilizational process. Without any doubt, the achievement of such understanding is crucial to man's continued habitation of the earth.

BETTY J. MEGGERS

Smithsonian Institution
Washington, D.C.
25 April 1968

Preface

This volume introduces a series of studies on the process of formation of the American peoples, on the causes of their unequal development, and on the possibilities for self-advancement that are open to the most backward among them.* Its objective is the construction of a new scheme of sociocultural development. While the attempt to synthesize sociocultural evolution during the past ten thousand years may seem rash, it is an indispensable prerequisite to an understanding of the formation of the American peoples. In truth, it can be avoided only by leaving the underlying conceptual scheme inexplicit or by drawing upon classical evolutionary formulations that are clearly inadequate to explain the situations facing mankind today.

Actually, whether they recognize it or not, all social scientists operate on the basis of a global theory of historical process whenever they employ categories referring to evolutionary stages—such as slavery, feudalism, capitalism, or socialism—or concepts relating to universal processes of sociocultural change—such as agricultural revolution, mercantile revolution, or industrial revolution. These concepts are used by the majority of academic social scientists, including those who reject the possibility of recognizing evolutionary sequences. Although the Marxists support the validity of a general theory of historical process, they have contributed little to its refinement because of their predisposition to orient most of their work toward the exemplification of classical Marxist theses. Meanwhile,

---

* Succeeding volumes are provisionally entitled *The Americas and Civilization* (the English edition will be published in 1969 by E. P. Dutton of New York), *The Latin American Dilemma,* and *The Brazilian Challenge.*

recent decades have seen the accumulation of copious archeological, ethno-graphical, and historical material describing human societies of diverse types, as well as the appearance of specialized studies on processes of cultural change and on specific lines of sociocultural evolution, all of which make a reformation of general evolutionary theory not only pos-sible but mandatory.

In spite of the obvious urgency of reexamining the theoretical basis of existing cultural evolutionary schemes, we might not have embarked on the task had it not become impossible to avoid it. While analyzing the causes of unequal development achieved by contemporary American na-tions, it became necessary to examine populations that represent the most divergent levels of development, and for which a great deal of reliable information is available. These include hunting-and-gathering tribes, agri-cultural groups just beginning to adopt sedentary life, populations that have taken the first steps toward state structure and social stratification into economic classes, urban civilizations based on irrigation agriculture and metallurgy and, finally, nations at different levels of integration into mercantile civilization and, increasingly, into modern industrial technol-ogy. How can we classify the indigenous peoples, who ranged from high civilizations to hunting-and-gathering bands and who reacted to the Euro-pean Conquest in terms of the level of development they had achieved? In relation to them and to the Europeans, where do we put the Africans who were taken from societies at different levels of development and brought to America as slave labor? How do we classify the Europeans who presided over the Conquest? Did the Iberians, who arrived first, and the Nordics, who followed and came to dominate extensive areas, create the same type of sociocultural formation? Finally, how can we classify the American national societies so as to distinguish their degrees of incorpo-ration into the way of life of agrarian-mercantile civilization and subse-quently of industrial civilization? The answer to these and many other questions of an equally crucial nature required the elaboration of a general theory of evolutionary process that would provide both a precise definition of the characteristics of successive phases and a more satisfactory explana-tion of the ways in which "out-of-phase" societies interact in the total system.

Our studies of the causes for inequality between American societies have not only made the elaboration of such a theory necessary, they have also facilitated its execution by providing both a non-European analytical perspective and an extraordinarily broad factual foundation. The former has permitted us to observe and evaluate the Eurocentrism inherent in existing theories of cultural evolution; the latter, drawn from the copious Americanist bibliography as well as personal experience in the anthropological study of tribal and national societies, has familiarized us with societies that represent not only most stages of sociocultural evolution, but also nearly all possible situations involving the meeting and mixing of peoples. The result is the scheme of technological, social, and ideological evolution of human societies contained in the present volume. We hope that this attempt will contribute to an identification of the basic stages of technological development within the continuum of culural evolution, to an explanation of specific ways of life in terms of the sociocultural formations that can be correlated with these evolutionary advances, to a recognition of the dynamic forces that are responsible for the sequence of stages and formations and, finally, to the definition of those conditions under which the process of transformation from one stage to another will be accelerated or retarded, or will lead to regression and stagnation. It is offered as a preliminary formulation rather than a final product, in recognition of the fact that further elaboration and refinement is dependent on the critical examination of other specialists.

In our view, the major shortcomings of this work consist in the bibliographic sources employed, and in the absence of a comparison of our views with those of previous authors. The bibliographical deficiency can be explained, although not justified, by the necessity of working without access either to good library facilities or to specialists in relevant fields and by the magnitude of the theme, which makes impossible an exhaustive examination of published sources relevant to the varying evolutionary stages and the innumerable cultures representing them. We hope that experts will excuse factual errors that may exist and, instead, concentrate their attention on the effort that has been made to interrelate stages and cultures and to discern their dynamics, and that criticism will be directed toward the theoretical contributions of the work rather than the specific examples cited for illustration.

The second shortcoming stems from a conscious decision. Our objective in preparing the present work was to provide as succinct as possible a formulation of the process of sociocultural evolution, with the consequence that erudite digressions that would have complicated and lengthened the text without adding to its intrinsic merit have been avoided. Specialists in the history of ideas will find in the Introduction to the Bibliography a review of the theoretical sources that have been particularly helpful.

Two additional bibliographic peculiarities will be noticed by specialists. First, we have drawn upon sources usually avoided by anthropologists on the ground that they are philosophical works or Marxist tracts. Frankly, however, we have found such works as useful as the more traditional academic sources, and occasionally more so because they fill a vacuum created by the efforts of anthropologists to avoid polemic by reducing crucial questions of human destiny to minor technicalities. Second, an exhaustive list of primary sources relating to the American peoples has not been provided, partly because such compilations are available elsewhere (e.g., Steward, 1946–1950; Baldus, 1954; Pericot García, 1962), and partly because a lengthy compilation, arranged by culture areas, is contained in another volume in this series, *As Américas e a Civilização*.

In conclusion, I should like to note that the present study has been made possible by the support of the Universidad de la República Oriental del Uruguay, which has provided me with a professorial appointment. It is also a pleasure to record my appreciation to Betty J. Meggers who, during translation of the text from Portuguese to English, made a number of suggestions for its improvement, and to Berta Ribeiro, who provided indispensable assistance and encouragement throughout the preparation of this work.

D.R.

Montevideo
1 February 1968

Contents

Illustrations

Introduction

In recent years, most anthropologists have readopted an evolutionary point of view, but have rephrased it in multilinear terms and disassociated it from the more conjectural earlier attempts to trace the origin of customs and institutions. There is not yet available, however, a global scheme for the stages of sociocultural evolution that is based on the most recent contributions from archeology, ethnology, and history—one that permits the placement of any society, whether living or extinct, into the continuum of sociocultural development.

The absence of such a scheme creates at least four kinds of deformation in social science theory. First, there is a tendency to apply theories of limited scope to problems like social development and modernization, which by their very nature require a broader and more comprehensive handling. Second, studies of cultural dynamics—especially those involving acculturation—are approached on the level of microanalysis, which contributes practically nothing to the knowledge of the processes by which cultural traditions are shaped and by which ethnic groups are formed and transformed. Third, functional studies are given prominence, obliging anthropologists to formulate theoretical explanations in terms of the interaction between elements present within each culture, and depriving them of the advantage inherent in the search for generalizations in the older diachronic perspective. Fourth, a theory of sociocultural evolution is implicit in many studies without being openly discussed or exposed to critical examination. Furthermore, even studies explicitly based on cultural evolutionary methodology are frequently formulated within such narrow limits that they do not provide a causal explanation of cultural dynamics, nor do they lead to the formulation of theories that explain the composition and interaction of contemporary societies as the result of long and complicated historical processes.

The filling of this theoretical gap, although obviously too large a task for one person, motivates this preliminary formulation of a theory of sociocultural evolution. It will focus on the evolution of human societies during the last ten millenia, in other words, since the appearance of the first agricultural communities. Earlier stages will be considered only to the minimal degree necessary to lay the foundation for later developments.

Theoretical Postulates

The history of human societies during the past ten millenia can be explained in terms of successive technological revolutions and civilizational processes, by means of which the majority of mankind has passed from a generalized hunting-and-gathering condition to diverse modes of subsistence, social organization, and self-explanation. Although these ways of life differ widely in cultural content, their variation is not arbitrary because of the underlying existence of three orders of imperatives. The first is the cumulative character of technological progress, which advances from simpler to more complex forms in an irreversible sequence. The second is the reciprocal relations between the technological equipment employed by a society in dealing with its natural environment and the size of its population, as well as the way in which those relations are organized both internally and with other societies. The third is the interaction of the forces used to control nature and to organize human relations with the rest of the culture; namely, the standardized ways of producing and thinking that are manifested materially in artifacts and property, behaviorally in social conduct, and ideologically in symbolic communication and the formulation of social experience into bodies of knowledge, beliefs, and values.

The existence of these three orders of interacting imperatives—technological, social, and ideological—means that a classification of evolutionary stages based on technological distinctions should bring to light complementary sequences of patterns in social organization and ideological configuration. The result should be a general evolutionary typology valid for all three imperatives, although derived primarily from the first of them. Such a typology should make it possible to fit all human societies into a limited number of structural categories, which in turn can be seriated into a sequence of more general evolutionary stages.

There is a high degree of agreement among students that the technological imperative exercises a determinative influence over the social and ideological aspects of culture and that progressive stages of technological evolution can be discerned. It is also generally agreed that the technological, social, and ideological sectors of a society are interconnected. There is much less unanimity regarding the possibility of equating these patterns of relationship with evolutionary stages that combine a certain level of technological development with specific features of social organization and particular kinds of ideological configuration. To many observers, the possible number of sociocultural responses to a particular technological system seems too large or too arbitrary to make a correlation between them practical, or to permit the creation of a universally applicable typology. Other students, while admitting the possibility of arriving at such a framework of stages, consider that it would have no operative value because universal stages would have to be formulated in such generic terms that they would be "neither very arguable nor very useful" (Steward, 1955, p. 17).

Even if this were true, however, the elaboration of a global scheme of sociocultural evolution is justifiable in terms of its value in explaining cultural dynamics. It is highly probable, moreover, that such a scheme would have a practical value, since it would permit the subdivision of sociocultural evolution into segments, each possessing specific characteristics relevant to concrete situations. Actually, as long as this kind of general perspective is missing, social scientists cannot frame problems that will lead to an understanding of the relationships between the concrete level of historical, archeological, and ethnographical studies and the abstract level of anthropological and sociological explanations. A general theory of sociocultural evolution is also a prerequisite to the elaboration of scientific generalizations from analysis of synchronic or functional relationships.

The basic concept underlying theories of sociocultural evolution is that human societies, over long periods of time, were affected by two simultaneous and mutually complementary processes, one of them responsible for diversification and the other for homogenization. Under the influence of the former, societies tend to multiply their population contingents, to expand the ethnic entities into which they agglutinate, and to diversify their cultural heritages. Because of the second process, however, this diversification does not lead to increasing differentiation between human groups, but rather to a homogenization of ways of life via the fusion of ethnic entities into ever larger units and the development of their cultural characteristics along parallel lines.

The first process, diversifying in character, is a response to the differing requirements of ecological adaptation, which impart unique qualities to each culture by channeling it toward specialization to a particular environment. It is also a consequence of the impact of unique historical events, which deflect the path of development. These individual qualities, although relevant to an explanation of the content of a particular society, are only of concern in an examination of the evolutionary process when they represent general modes of human adaptation utilizable by other societies.

The second process, which is integrating and homogenizing in character, is sociocultural evolution. It could be said that sociocultural evolution proceeds by a realization of the limited possibilities for response to similar fundamental imperatives under similar conditions. This leads to the repetition of cultural forms and to the creation of uniformities in structure, which make it possible to establish a universal typology.

Examination of the varied composition of those human societies for which we have adequate documentation reveals that they can be categorized according to their degree of efficiency in achieving a mastery over nature. This categorization implies the existence of a developmental process that, while it does not operate with the same intensity on all societies, neither does it act arbitrarily. On the contrary, it is both regulated and directional because of the existence of a series of causal forces, including one general imperative and three basic contingencies that are extra-cultural in character, as well as several factors of a cultural nature.

The general imperative is the uniformity of the natural environment within which man operates, and which obliges him to adjust to physico-chemical and biological factors that are not modifiable by culture. The leveling effect of this imperative is most evident in technology which, because of its direct involvement with nature, must of necessity respond to its requirements. As a consequence of this imperative, we find in all cultures a minimum body of objective knowledge and a standardized means of production, and these exercise a determinative influence on the other aspects of the culture.

The three basic contingencies of an extra-cultural nature combine with this general imperative to stamp all cultures with similar guidelines. All three can be subsumed under the label "human nature." The first kind stems from man's biological structure, and sets him apart from other species; it includes intelligence, flexibility, individuality, and sociability—traits that result from the process of biological evolution. This biological uniformity is reflected in the universal development of cultural norms of action upon the environment for the extraction of those materials essential to human survival and reproduction (collecting, hunting, fishing, etc.). Secondly, there are the contingencies of group living, which require the creation of cultural guidelines for the maintenance of group solidarity (family, kinship, clan, etc.) and for economic production (division of labor, stratification, etc.). Thirdly, there are contingencies of a psychological nature, which are more difficult to define, but which reflect the essential unity of the neuropsychological and mental structure of human beings, and which lead to independent discovery of similar responses to the same kinds of challenges.

In addition to the general imperative and these three contingencies—all of an extra-cultural nature—there is another imperative that is cultural. This is the uniquely human capacity for symbolic communication, which is responsible for enveloping social life in a fabric of cultural tradition transmitted from generation to generation, and which makes all developments dependent on the characteristics of the pre-existing heritage.

Within the limitations set by these various factors, the accumulation of communal knowledge and the exercise of options have produced human culture in all its variations. The necessity of developing within this restrictive framework makes cultural evolution directional. Instead of always beginning anew, human activities are linked across generations into evolutionary sequences that are equivalent to those in biological evolution, but are both more variable and more uniform than the latter. Nature, evolving by genetic mutation, cannot return to an earlier state and is held to a relatively slow rate of transformation. Culture, on the other hand, evolves by the addition of bodies of information and ways of acting, and is disseminated by learning, thus making possible rapid change, the spread of new ideas with minimal spacial or temporal limitations, and the creation of increasingly larger and more homogeneous configurations.

The anthropological literature exhaustively demonstrates the universal character of these factors as well as the uniformity of the cultural response by documenting the presence of the same classes of elements in the basic structure of different cultures. This repetitive character of the responses made during the course of history to the causal challenges that confront all societies is attested by the occurrence of many similar forms of social stratification, political institutions, religious behavior, etc. There is also ample evidence not only for the existence of a succession of technological systems—based on the same physico-chemical and biological principles, but endowed with increasing efficiency both in productivity and in the capacity to support ever larger groups of people—but for the power of some societies to gain domination over others. In short, all the data indicate that the evolutionary process must be viewed as both homogenizing and directional.

Sociocultural evolution has been considered thus far as an internal process of transformation that operates within the extra-cultural limitations already mentioned. In reality, however, cultures are not developed and maintained in isolation, but in a continuous interrelation with one another. Consequently, the internal creativity responsible for cultural innovations is supplemented by diffusion, which adds new traits, and by social compulsions of external origin, which may alter the course of evolutionary development. Although it is possible to isolate conceptually the variations that result from specialized ecological adaptation, the same is not true of variations brought about by diffusion or external pressures. The importance of the latter two factors is so great, however, that a satisfactory theory of sociocultural evolution must recognize their existence.

The present analysis attempts to show: (1) that the development of societies and cultures is regulated by an orientational principle originating from the cumulative development of productive and military technology; (2) that certain advances in this technology represent quantitative changes of a radical character that make it possible to distinguish stages or phases of sociocultural evolution; and (3) that these progressive technological stages correlate with necessary, and consequently uniform, alterations in social organization and ideological configuration.

The attribution of determinative power to technological innovations of a productive or military nature does not exclude the presence of other dynamic forces. On the contrary, over short periods of time social organization can bring about a realization of the potentialities inherent in technological advances, and a beneficial or adverse influence can also be exerted by ideological elements (such as scientific knowledge) on technology and through the latter, on social structure. Examples include the dynamic roles played by the phenomena of solidarity (Kropotkin, 1955) or conflict between economic classes (Marx, 1967); or between social units structured around cultural loyalties, such as national ethnic groups (Znaniecki, 1944) or religious groups (M. Weber, 1948). Even though these forms of solidarity and conflict are linked with technology, they are not reducible to technology, nor is their variety of form and function explainable in its terms. White (1949, p. 382) expressed this same point when he asserted that "every social system rests upon and is determined by a technological system. But every technological system functions *within* a social system, and therefore is conditioned by it."

Recognition of the interaction between these various orders of determinants makes it possible to achieve a realistic comprehension of the process of sociocultural evolution, which combines a more abstract global perspective with complementary perspectives of an historical nature, derived from the interplay between currents of cultural diffusion and acculturative pressures. Such a conceptual integration makes it unnecessary to choose between the relativistic doctrines of diffusionism, parallelism, and convergence, and the more radical evolutionistic explanations, which are based on the psychic unity of mankind or an exaggeration of the frequency of independent invention. Adoption of such a broad analytic perspective also permits us to view the diversification and homogenization of societies and cultures as resulting from local inventions (the rarer alternative), from the acquisition of advances diffused from elsewhere, and from responses to stresses created either by pressures for ecological adaptation or by the necessity to maintain an integration between the various cultural segments.

Recognition of the developmental phenomena that promote the homogeneity of cultural configurations on a global scale is facilitated by creating the concept of the civilizational process. Reference to such a concept also permits evaluation both of the differential effects of adaptation to specific ecological and historical situations, and of the degree to which the posing of alternative responses to similar basic challenges is permitted. This concept is in some ways similar to the cultural circles and strata of the diffusionists (Schmidt and Koppers, 1924; Graebner, 1924; Montandon, 1934), to culture area formulations (Wissler, 1938; Murdock, 1951; Kroeber, 1939, 1944), and even to cultural typologies (Redfield, 1956;

Linton, 1936; Benedict, 1934). All of these, however, have an anti-evolutionistic bias, as well as other limitations. Complexes of traits that compose the *Kulturkreise*, for example, are fanciful in character; the culture areas are tied to geography; the search for culture types is often psychological in emphasis. Our approach is closer to the culture type concept as reformulated by Steward (1955, Ch. 11), who also made an effort to supersede earlier notions of culture areas and evolutionary stages. Our general civilizational process, however, overcomes the causal limitations of Steward's culture type, since it combines the concepts of technological revolution as the basic causal factor, sociocultural formations as theoretical models of cultural response to these revolutions, and civilizations as concrete historical entities that are crystallized out of the formations.

This perspective also achieves a higher plane of abstraction than the one on which Steward operated, and this makes it possible to examine diachronically large groups or classes of societies such as the nomadic pastoral hordes and the irrigation civilizations. This higher level of generalization obviously requires a correspondingly larger degree of abstraction in the definition of the diagnostic traits of each formation. It remains to be seen whether this will permit both the derivation of generalizations that can explain global sociocultural evolution and the classification into a scale of general evolutionary stages of the individual societies that are the concrete components. It is our belief that even under the limitations of this preliminary study, we can demonstrate this to be the case.

Conceptual Scheme

The greatest difficulty confronting an attempt to formulate a global evolutionary scheme is the need to combine different temporal and functional approaches, and to invest them with the appropriate degree of congruity and reliability, so as to permit comprehension both of the grand current of human cultural evolution and of the tumultuous steps in its historical progress and regression. In the following pages we will attempt to make explicit the foundations and limitations within which we propose to formulate such a general evolutionary scheme. The analysis will involve several levels of abstraction and make use of the concepts of *general civilizational process*, whose meaning approximates that of A. Weber's (1935) "civilizing process"; of *individual civilizational processes,* with the significance that Sorokin (1937–1941) gave to the term "cultural supersystems"; of *technological revolutions,* but in a more restricted sense than that given to the concept of "cultural revolutions" by Childe (1936, 1951) and White (1959); of *sociocultural formations,* with the meaning that Marx (1904, 1965, 1967) gave to the expression "socio-economic formations"; of *structural models and types* in the sense of M. Weber (1954); and finally of *cultural historical configurations,* with a significance close to that of Steward's (1955) "cultural types." We will also make use of the concepts of *progress, regression, stagnation, historical incorporation,* and *evolutionary acceleration* in special ways that will be precisely defined. It will also be necessary to redefine, in terms of the proposed conceptualization, the notions of *civilization,* of *genuine* and *spurious culture* (Sapir, 1924); of *cultural autonomy* and *cultural anachronism* (Ogburn, 1926); of *cultural traumatization, restoration,* and *crystallization* (Foster, 1962); of *acculturation* and *deculturation;* and of *ethnos, macro-ethnos,* and *national ethnos,* as well as sociological concepts like *assimilation, development,* and *modernization.*

We conceive of sociocultural evolution as a temporal pattern of alteration in the ways of life of human groups. This alteration is created by the impact of successive technological revolutions (agricultural, industrial, etc.) on specific societies, tending to transform them from one evolutionary stage to another, or from one sociocultural formation to another. Sociocultural formations are conceptual models of social life, each of which combines a specific level of development in productive technology with a generic form of social regulation and with an ideological configuration that represents a greater or lesser degree of lucidity and rationality.

Each sociocultural formation is thus a particular constellation of certain aspects of mode of environmental adaptation, certain attributes of social organization, and certain qualities of world view. These three orders of phenomena correspond to three systems: adaptive, associative, and ideological. The *adaptive system* is composed of the cultural means of manipulating nature for the production and reproduction of the material requirements of a society. The *associative system* includes standardized means of regulating interpersonal relations that involve subsistence activities and biological reproduction. At certain stages of sociocultural evolution, tendencies toward the institutionalization of social life beyond the family and of elementary kinds of division of labor express themselves in new forms of property, in social stratification in terms of differentiated roles in the productive process, and in the emergence of regulative institutions of a political, religious, or educational character. The third order of elements making up a sociocultural formation is its *ideological system,* which includes not only abstract knowledge about techniques of production and social norms, but all forms of symbolic communication—such as language, explicit formulations of knowledge, bodies of beliefs, and systems of values—which are developed to explain and justify a people's behavior and way of life. These three systems comprise the culture of a society. In a sufficiently homogeneous group of societies, they assume a generic character that permits the recognition of a culture type, as in the case of pastoral societies or, when there is geographic continuity, of a culture area; for example, the indigenous horticulturists of the South American tropical forest.

The concept of *sociocultural formation* applies to a higher level of abstraction; one in which, for example, all hunting-and-gathering tribal groups are combined into a single category. As a result, the degree of specificity characterizing the adaptive, associative, and ideological systems that correspond to a particular sociocultural formation must be relatively low, although not so low as to make the scheme valueless for classificatory purposes. The great difficulty in constructing theoretical paradigms of sociocultural formations is thus the recognition of distinctive aspects, which because of their crucial nature and their influential role constitute a minimum definition. An allied problem arises from the wide variation in cultural traditions, which makes it improbable that all the diagnostic traits will occur in every society assigned to a given formation. Rather, incomplete representation is likely to be more frequent than a faithful reproduction of the theoretical model.

The ideal way to define sociocultural formations would be to identify a body of homogeneous diagnostic traits that not only represent the adaptive, associative, and ideological systems and traverse all the sociocultural formations, but which also embrace all significant modifications. This ideal cannot be realized, however, because of the range of variation in the content of each culture. As a consequence, each stage or formation must be defined in its own terms and without the requirement that the same kinds of elements must form part of the definition of an earlier or later stage. Even such specific definitions cannot be constructed with the desirable degree of homogeneity, however, because the choice of criteria is limited by practical considerations, including ease of correlation with designations prevalent in the classical bibliography on the subject. We will, therefore, draw upon existing terms that refer to productive activities (hunting-and-gathering, pastoral, agricultural, rural craftsman, irrigation, industrial), to social stratification, and labor and property relations (undifferentiated—as opposed to stratified—collectivistic, privatistic, slavistic, mercantile, capitalistic, socialistic), to political entities (tribe, horde, village, chiefdom, state, empire, colony), and to ideological systems and special attributes thereof (theocratic, salvationistic, despotic, revolutionary, evolutionary, modernizing).

The theoretical construction of sociocultural formations also presents two additional difficulties, both of which derive from the abstract nature of the analytical categories. The first is the reconciliation of their developmental aspect, as stages in an evolutionary continuum, with their nonchronological nature, which permits the coexistence of societies that are classifiable into the most disparate evolutionary stages. This ambivalent situation, which led Huxley (1955) to characterize evolutionary stages as "nonsynchronic homotaxa," creates special problems since relations between contrasting formations frequently produce ambiguous results in the form of societies incorporating traits that normally correspond to distinct "moments" in evolution. This frequently results from the implantation of modern industries in backward areas, as with the recently pacified Xavante Indians of Brazil who, although primitive in most respects, use metal tools. Such situations, far from invalidating the deterministic nature of the evolutionary framework, help to confirm it. They require us, however, to consider in all their complexity not only the autonomous processes of development and the effects of diffusion and acculturation, but also the consequences of both kinds of phenomena for the peoples that experience them.

The second problem stems from the dynamic nature of the sociocultural formations, which makes them more comparable to a directional continuum than to a series of discrete stages. As a result, it becomes necessary to recognize an incipient (formative) aspect that may be little differentiated from the preceding formation, and a mature (florescent) aspect that results from intensification of the diagnostic characteristics. Thus when a transition takes place between two successive stages, the florescent aspect of the earlier one may often be difficult to distinguish from the formative aspect of the later one. Such confusion is inevitable, and is characteristic not only of evolutionary situations, but also of societies undergoing cultural trauma as a result of external pressures. The recognition of such a transitional, incipient stage, however, permits the classification and incorporation into the proposed typology of those societies in which archaic survivals are combined with new qualities that have not yet assumed a dominant role.

Only under exceptional conditions do societies move continually upward in evolution, passing through all the successive stages. Their course is usually interrupted by a variety of factors, which may lead either to stagnation and cultural regression, or to cycles of advances and declines. In fact, there seems to be a correlation between the maturity of a formation and a tendency toward regression. This is explainable in some cases by the fact that maturity coincides with saturation in the exploitation of the creative potential of the technology, and in others by expansionistic tendencies that emerge with maturation. The latter bring about extremely tense dominance relations, the oppressive nature of which can rupture a sociocultural constellation by reversing the roles of the dominated peoples and the dominating center. This situation leads to the development of militarism and colonialism at a certain point in the maturation of all advanced formations, and thus eliminates these features from inclusion among the general diagnostic traits used to define a specific evolutionary stage. Their universality, however, makes them of decisive importance in the general study of one basic motivating force of evolution; namely, the acculturative social compulsion that is primarily responsible for the creation and modification of ethnic entities.

All concrete societies are continually undergoing alterations, as a consequence both of interaction between their constituent parts and of influence from other societies and, therefore, they inevitably exhibit more or less severe disconformities. In this respect, they differ from the conceptual formulations, which express an ideal state of maturity and equilibrium seldom encountered in real situations. Conditions commonly classified as "structural duality" reflect a similar kind of disconformity, resulting from differences in the rhythms of transformation in various sectors of a culture.

All of this means that classification of concrete societies into evolutionary schemes can only be done after they have been conceptually stripped of any unique aspects, leaving only those features diagnostic of the model for each formation. The focus must also be on long periods of time so that the significance of alterations can more easily be perceived.

Technological Revolutions and Civilizational Processes

The concept of technological revolution is employed here to designate those transformations in man's ability to exploit nature or to make war that are prodigious enough to produce qualitative alterations in the whole way of life of societies. Consequently, it is assumed that the unleashing of each technological revolution, or the multiplication of its effects in different sociocultural contexts via the civilizational processes, will tend to correlate with the emergence of new sociocultural formations.

Most students accept the classification of Childe (1936), which distinguishes three "cultural revolutions." The first is the *Agricultural Revolution*, which introduced the cultivation of plants and the domestication of animals into the subsistence system, transforming man's situation from that of an exploiter of nature's spontaneous bounty to that of an active agent of food production. The succeeding *Urban Revolution*, which stemmed from innovations in subsistence production and the invention of metallurgy and writing, led to the internal dichotomization of societies into rural and urban segments, to social stratification into classes, and to other profound alterations in social life and cultural heritage. Finally, the *Industrial Revolution*, which began in western Europe with the harnessing of inanimate energy to operate mechanical devices, was responsible for new and fundamental changes in social stratification, political organization, and world view.

When an effort was made to correlate technological revolutions with sociocultural formations, however, it became obvious that a larger number of revolutions had to be recognized. As a consequence, the Urban Revolution is followed in our scheme by the *Irrigation Revolution*, which provided the technological basis for the appearance of the first regional civilizations. Significant technological advances include construction of large canals for irrigation and navigation, new types of watercraft, systems of roads, and cities with large public buildings (pyramids, temples, and palaces), as well as ideographic writing, systems of weights and measures, and scientific developments, especially in the realms of mathematics and astronomy. Following

Figure 1 Basic sequences of sociocultural evolution in terms of technological revolutions, civilizational processes, and sociocultural formations. The italicized formations result from processes of historical incorporation and are the most significant of the many that have been produced in this way.

TECHNOLOGICAL REVOLUTIONS	GENERAL CIVILIZATIONAL PROCESSES
I Agricultural Revolution	1 Agricultural Revolution
	2 Pastoral Expansion
II Urban Revolution	3 Urban Revolution
	4 Slavistic Expansion
	5 Second Pastoral Expansion
III Irrigation Revolution	6 Irrigation Revolution
IV Metallurgical Revolution	7 Metallurgical Revolution
V Pastoral Revolution	8 Pastoral Revolution
VI Mercantile Revolution	9 Mercantile Revolution
	10 Capitalistic Expansion
VII Industrial Revolution	11 Industrial Revolution
	12 Socialistic Expansion
VIII Thermonuclear Revolution	

SOCIOCULTURAL FORMATIONS	HISTORICAL EXAMPLES
Undifferentiated Horticultural Villages	Jarmo (5th mil. B.C.) Tupinambá (16th century)
Nomadic Pastoral Hordes	Guaikurú (18th century) Kirghiz (20th century)
Rural Craftsman States (Collectivist type)	Urartu (10th century B.C.) Mochica (2nd century B.C.)
Rural Craftsman States (Privatistic type)	Phoenicians (2nd mil. B.C.) Kushan (5th century B.C.)
Nomadic Pastoral Chiefdoms	Hyksos (18th cent. B.C.) Huns (3–5th century)
Theocratic Irrigation Empires	Egypt (3rd mil. B.C.) Inca (15th century)
Mercantile Slavistic Empires	Greece (5th century B.C.) Rome (1st century B.C.)
Despotic Salvationist Empires	Islam (7th century) Ottoman (15th century)
Salvationistic Mercantile Empires	Iberia (16th century) Russia (16th century)
Slavistic Colonies	Brazil (16th century) Cuba (18th century)
Capitalistic Mercantile Empires	Holland (17th century) England (17th century)
Trading Colonies	Indonesia (19th century) Guianas (20th century)
Immigrant Colonies	North America (17th century) Australia (19th century)
Imperialistic Industrial Powers	England (19th century) United States (20th century)
Neo-Colonial Dependencies	Brazil (20th century) Venezuela (20th century)
Socialistic Revolutionary Nations	USSR (1917) China (1949)
Socialistic Evolutionary Nations	Sweden (1945) England (1965)
Nationalistic Modernizing States	Egypt (1953) Algeria (1962)

Future Societies

it, we have added the *Metallurgical Revolution,* which equates generally with the Iron Age of archeological sequences. During its course, the alphabet and decimal notation were invented, and iron forging, the manufacture of tools, and coinage were perfected and diffused. With the succeeding *Pastoral Revolution,* some of the earlier innovations were applied to harnessing animals for traction and warfare, and to improvements in the use of wind and water for productive purposes. In our view, furthermore, the Industrial Revolution was preceded by the *Mercantile Revolution,* which was based on the technology of oceanic navigation and firearms, and was responsible for the breakdown of European feudalism. Finally, we have recognized the *Thermonuclear Revolution,* which is underway at the present time with the application of electronics, atomic energy, automation, laser beams, etc. It holds potentialities for the transformation of human life as radical as those of any previous technological revolution.

In summary, therefore, we recognize eight technological revolutions that are characterized by major transformations in productive capacity and military might, and which lead to fundamental modifications in the adaptive, associative, and ideological systems of the people that experience them, whether they do so indirectly or directly. Yet without a recognition of the complementary concept of the civilizational process, this series of technological revolutions is not sufficient to explain the whole evolutionary process. The reason for this is that it is not the invention itself that produces consequences, but rather its dissemination into various sociocultural contexts and its application to different sectors of production. Thus, for each technological revolution there may be one or more civilizational processes through which its potentialities for the transformation of material life and the transfiguration of sociocultural formations are realized (Figure 1).

The first of these civilizational processes spread the technology of plant domestication, destroying the nomadic hunting-and-gathering way of life, and giving rise to a new sociocultural formation, the *Undifferentiated Horticultural Villages.* Under the influence of the second civilizational process, which corresponds to animal domestication and the functional specialization of some groups in this substistence activity (Pastoral Expansion), another formation was generated that can be termed *Nomadic Pastoral Hordes.*

The Urban Revolution incorporates the third, fourth, and fifth civilizational processes. The third corresponds to the rise of cities and states, to the stratification of societies into social classes, to the first experiments in irrigation agriculture, and to copper and bronze metallurgy, ideographic writing, numbers, and the calendar. It resulted in the crystallization of the *Rural Craftsman States* formation. Maturation of the fourth civilizational process is expressed by the adoption of private property and the enslavement of the labor force in some Rural Craftsman States, which transformed them from a *Collectivistic* to a *Privatistic* form. Finally, elaboration of certain technological developments, such as the use of copper and its application to pastoral activities, during the course of the fifth civilizational process (alternatively designated as the Second Pastoral Expansion), brought into existence the *Nomadic Pastoral Chiefdoms*.

Maturation of the basic technology that produced the Urban Revolution, especially that relating to the construction of large irrigation works, led to the Irrigation Revolution. With it came the sixth civilizational process, which created the first regional civilizations, the *Theocratic Irrigation Empires*, as a new sociocultural formation. The seventh civilizational process originated from the Metallurgical Revolution, based on generalization of technological innovations like iron forging. This permitted the development of a more productive agriculture in forested regions, the manufacture of a variety of new tools, and the improvement of sailing vessels. Other significant inventions were coinage, which facilitated external commerce, the phonetic alphabet, and decimal notation. This technological base led to the maturation of a new sociocultural formation in the form of the *Mercantile Slavistic Empires*.

The eighth civilizational process was set in motion by the Pastoral Revolution. It was founded on the application of certain elements of the same basic technology (especially forged iron) to production and warfare, including a generalized use of saddles, stirrups, and horseshoes (all of which increased the efficiency of animals for riding and traction) and swords and rigid armor. These technological improvements led to the development of a messianic expansionistic movement among some of the Nomadic Pastoral Chiefdoms, which attacked areas occupied by early feudal civilizations and incorporated them into *Despotic Salvationist Empires*.

The ninth civilizational process equates with the Mercantile Revolution and the first world civilizations. It gave rise to two sociocultural formations, the *Salvationistic Mercantile Empires* and their reciprocals, the *Slavis-*

tic Colonies. The tenth civilizational process reflects the progressive elaboration of this same technological revolution, and led to the appearance of the *Capitalistic Mercantile Empires* and two reciprocal formations, *Trading Colonies* and *Immigrant Colonies.* The Industrial Revolution brought about a restructuring into *Imperialistic Industrial Powers* and *Neo-Colonial Dependencies* under the influence of the eleventh civilizational process. Rational intervention or social planning constitutes the twelfth civilizational process, which created the *Socialistic Revolutionary, Socialistic Evolutionary,* and *Nationalistic Modernizing States.*

The emerging Thermonuclear Revolution, with its immense potential for transformation of the material life of peoples the world over, will accelerate the evolution of backward groups and produce new sociocultural formations. These *Future Societies* will probably render obsolete both existing types of social stratification and the dependence on warfare in international relations.

The conceptual framework proposed here makes it possible to distinguish between a *global civilizational process,* largely synonymous with sociocultural evolution, and general and individual civilizational processes, which are contained within the global process and contribute to its formation, but which also produce individual civilizations. The global view derives from the perspective provided by the present over the past. It permits us to appreciate retrospectively how varying particular cultural traditions, developed at different times and places, have become interlinked, interfertilizing, or destroying one another, but in so doing advancing a great cultural tradition and contributing to the creation of the universal human civilization now beginning to take shape.

The *general civilizational processes* correspond to generic evolutionary sequences resulting from the effects on the lives of diverse peoples of cultural innovations unleashed by a technological revolution. Dissemination of each of these processes causes racial mixture and cultural unification of divergent groups, and brings about new sociocultural formations, either by simple historical incorporation or by evolutionary acceleration. This occurred, for example, with the expansion of irrigation agriculture, which although it energized the lives of different groups in distinct places and at different times, remodeled their societies and cultures along similar general lines. In contrast, the *individual civilizational processes* as conceived here are concrete historical expressions of the general civilizational processes.

For example, the expansion of irrigation in Mesopotamia was an individual civilizational process, which led to the maturation of several local civilizations based on irrigation; parallel developments occurred both in Egypt and India.

This conceptual framework requires the redefinition of the concepts of ethnos (ethnic group) and civilization. *Civilizations* are the crystallizations of individual civilizational processes. Each civilization expands from its metropolitan centers, bringing the surrounding area under economic and political domination and cultural influence (e.g., the Egyptian, Aztec, and Greek civilizations). The *ethnos* (ethnic groups) are the operative units of the civilizational process, each of which corresponds to a unique human group united by a common language and culture (e.g., the Tupinambá or Germanic ethnic group). We can speak of a *national ethnos* when linguistic, cultural, and national political boundaries coincide, and of a *macro-ethnos* when such states expand to incorporate populations of different ethnic origins. An ethnos may be a hunting band, composed of family groups that move over a defined territory, or a national minority that is segregated by its common language and traditions, and has aspirations toward autonomy. Or it may be a group that preserves certain common integrative traditions and whose members are united by strong in-group loyalties, like the Gypsies or the Jews. When two or more such groups are combined by imperialistic domination in an attempt to amalgamate them into a larger entity, they form part of a macro-ethnos (e.g., Roman, Inca, or Spanish Colonial).

When conceived as a succession of general civilizational processes, sociocultural evolution has a progressive character that corresponds to man's rise from a tribal condition to modern national macro-societies. As conceptualized here, general civilizational processes are also evolutionary expansions by which progressively more complex sociocultural formations are produced. By contrast, individual civilizational processes are concrete historical expansions that may vitalize wide areas and crystallize into diverse civilizations, but which tend to have a cyclical history. Civilizations thus rise, fall into periods of regression or "dark ages," and rebuild themselves along similar lines—until the cycle is broken by the unfolding of a new general civilizational process, which in turn gives rise to specific civilizational processes from which a new type of civilization emerges.

Diffusion and acculturation studies achieve increased clarity when examined in terms of the individual civilizational processes. The concept of *diffusion* does not require special definition because it will be employed here in the usual sense; i.e., to refer to the direct or indirect transfer of cultural traits of any type without necessitating the subordination of the receiver by the donor. The concept of *acculturation,* however, will not be restricted to situations involving contact between autonomous cultural entities—which is the most common usage in the anthropological literature (e.g., Herskovits, 1938; Redfield and others, 1936; Beals, 1953; Barnett and others, 1954). If strictly adhered to, such a definition would limit application of the concept to intertribal relations, because only in such cases are the cultures autonomous and able to adopt foreign cultural traits without a loss of independence. In the interest of wider applicability, therefore, acculturation will be expanded here to include both the amalgamation of advanced cultural traditions and their expansion over less-developed cultural complexes.

Historical Incorporation and Evolutionary Acceleration

When viewed within the framework of a broad historical perspective, several aspects of cultural development become evident. Among them are the transitory character of institutions, the attitude displayed by various interests toward social change, and the progressive or regressive character of tensions prevalent in transitional societies. The difficulties inherent in dealing with problems of social dynamics on the basis of theories of limited scope and functionalist methodology—both of which attempt to explain sociocultural problems in terms of the interaction of constituent elements as though the societies did not have a past history, or on the assumption that all elements have an equal determinative potential—can be surmounted with the perspective provided by the civilizational processes. This perspective also helps to overcome the tendency to view the most highly developed societies of today as the ideal sociocultural system and the objective toward which all peoples are moving (e.g., Lerner, 1958; Balandier, Ed., 1956; Perroux, 1958; Gerschenkron, 1962; Eisenstadt, 1963a; Baran, 1957). In order to deal with such problems, several other concepts should be defined, among them historical incorporation, evolutionary acceleration, cultural stagnation, and historical backwardness or regression.

Historical incorporation will be used here to designate the process by which backward peoples are forcibly integrated into more highly evolved technological systems, with consequent loss of autonomy or even the destruction of their ethnic distinctness. This took place, for example, with the incorporation into colonial American slavistic formations of subjugated indigenous people and of transplanted African populations for slave labor in mines and on plantations. Thus the concept of incorporation refers both to situations that are of a regressive character from the standpoint of the enslaved ethnic entities, which may be traumatized or even destroyed, and to those of a progressive nature in the sense that they incorporate retarded peoples into more advanced socio-economic systems. The most significant characteristic of the process of historical incorporation is its reflex action, which inflicts loss of autonomy and the risk of ethnic disintegration on the incorporated groups.

The process of historical incorporation also includes cases in which a society suffers the indirect consequences of alterations produced in the adaptive systems of other societies. Although profound transformations of a progressive nature often take place, a dependent relationship is also inevitably established. This is a frequent result of the diffusion of products of the Industrial Revolution such as railroads and ports, which have "modernized" large sectors of the non-European world to make them more efficient producers of certain kinds of articles, but in so doing have also made these sectors increasingly dependent on the exporters of the industrial goods. Because of this process, the populations of Latin America extricated themselves from the status of colonial areas in a Salvationistic Mercantile formation, only to become Neo-Colonial Dependencies of Imperialistic Industrial formations.

The concept of *evolutionary acceleration* will be used to refer to progress that is achieved without loss of autonomy or ethnic identity. For example, a society may undergo a technological revolution as a result of internal creativity, or by the autonomous adoption of technological innovations achieved by other societies, or by a combination of the two. Other kinds of evolutionary acceleration occur in societies that were at one time subjugated by processes of historical incorporation, but which have regained their lost political autonomy, as was the case with the former colonial populations of North America. Evolutionary acceleration may also be produced by a political vanguard that operates in the name of the subordinate classes, and which brings about a restructuring of the society in accord with the interests

of the latter by removing forces hostile to the adoption and general application of a more efficient productive technology. In the same category, although less effective, are efforts to bring about socio-economic progress
through governmental programs of planned development, which are always directed toward the reinforcement of political and economic autonomy.

Viewed within this framework, the developed and underdeveloped peoples of the modern world do not represent distinct and unequally advanced
stages of cultural evolution. On the contrary, they are interacting and mutually complementary components of broad systems of domination, linked
by a symbiotic relationship that tends to perpetuate their status as poles of
progress and retardation within a single civilization. The developed societies
of the contemporary world are those that have integrated themselves into
industrial civilization by evolutionary acceleration. The underdeveloped
ones are those that were drawn in by historical incorporation as "external
proletariats," which are destined to provide not only the necessities of life
but prosperity for the developed peoples to which they are related.

Still to be defined are the concepts of *cultural stagnation* and *historical
regression*. The former refers to the condition of societies that remain without notable alterations in their way of life over long periods of time, during
which other societies advance. Examples are the pre-agricultural tribes and
tropical forest horticulturists of South America, which remained in the
same cultural stage for millennia while other peoples of the continent rose
to the level of urban civilization. Stagnation has been explained in terms
of anti-progressive elements, such as the oppressive or nonstimulating condition of a humid forest environment; or, contrarywise, its generous productivity, which offers no incentive to increased efforts. It has also been
attributed to the absence of dynamic factors like domesticable animals, and
as a consequence, the absence of aggressive pastoral groups; or to isolation
from external contacts. Another explanation has been that extreme specialization brings about so satisfactory an adaptation to the environment
that societies achieving it are rendered incapable of further advance.

Among the numerous examples of stagnation are certain super-specialized cultures of the arctic regions or the steppes, which represent generic
modes of adaptation by societies that are very diverse in other characteristics. Groups like the polar Eskimo or the Timbira of the Brazilian scrub
forest (cerrado) exhibit extreme cultural specialization toward a particular

type of environment. This adaptation was achieved by deviating from rather than following a path of progressive cultural development. The excellence of some of these adaptations, which permit creation, reproduction, and expansion of human communities under highly adverse ecological conditions, does not alter the fact that the complexes they represent are marginal and consequently condemned at a certain stage in general cultural evolution either to retardation or to stagnation. The correctness of this analysis is shown by the fact that both in the arctic and in the scrub forest modern scientific technology has brought about much more efficient adaptations, evidenced by increase in size of the populations that can be supported.

Although it is possible to recognize several secondary agents of stagnation, the primary explanations are historical and ecological. Stagnating cultures are relevant to a general study of the civilizational process only as representatives of peoples still outside its sphere of influence, but who will inevitably be drawn in, either by historical incorporation or by evolutionary acceleration, depending on the conditions under which they enter into contact with more advanced peoples who penetrate their territories.

Examples of sociocultural *regression* can also be explained by a variety of factors. Some are the result of the impact of a more highly developed society on more backward peoples, who avoid ethnic disintegration by retreating to an inhospitable region where their former system of adaptation does not function efficiently. This happened to a number of New World peoples when Europeans invaded their territories. Regression can also result from internal trauma like insurrection and destruction of the old social order, if a new and more progressive one does not emerge. Among many such cases is the situation in ancient Egypt around 2200 B.C., when Memphis was paralyzed and fell into decline, never to flourish again. Another is Haiti following its independence; here, only a complete and intentional reorganization of the entire social structure, which was beyond its capabilities, would have permitted the creation of an economic structure as efficient as the former slavistic colonialism, and able at the same time to fulfill the aspirations of the population for liberty and progress.

Another factor leading to regression is reactionary behavior on the part of the dominant class which, when menaced in its hegemony, adopts measures that have an involutional effect. For example, the obsession to retain domination over a slavistic context produced the Spartan caricature of Greek culture. Similarly, both Nazi Germany and Fascist Italy were disfigured by their desperate efforts to suppress emergent socialistic movements, and by their transformation into centers of imperialistic domination. All such anti-historical interruptions slide into decadent militaristic and despotic regimes, which first degrade the social and cultural life of their people, and subsequently propel them into disastrous wars. A further cause of cultural regression is over-utilization of an efficient technology like irrigation agriculture, which at the level of saturation becomes destructive of the environment. This occurred in the valleys of the Indus, Tigris and Euphrates, Hwang-ho, and Yangtse, where millions of hectares of agricultural land were lost by erosion or by increasing alkalinity or salinity of the soil resulting from deficient drainage during long periods of flood cultivation (Revelle, 1963).

The principal cause of cultural regression, however, is exhaustion of the potentialities of a sociocultural formation, which toward the end of its existence solidifies the social structure and creates conflicts between classes. When this occurs, continued social life depends on the development of despotic institutions for strict control of the labor force and for repression of lower class rebellions. In this form of regression, a special role is played by the attacks of culturally backward peoples, who succeed in defeating and subjugating more advanced societies that have been made vulnerable by their structural rigidity and internal crises. This situation gives rise to one of the most important forms of sociocultural regression; namely, the plunge of relatively advanced societies into so-called "dark ages." Such is our conceptualization of feudalism; we do not view it as a sociocultural formation or an evolutionary stage, but rather as a regression produced by disintegration of the associative, the centralized political and administrative, and the commercial systems within an area once integrated by a civilization, so that it falls back into a subsistence economy. When a feudal regression takes place, the cities also lose their dynamism, and the erudite cultural tradition that once radiated from them tends to be replaced by an orally transmitted folk tradition. The arts and crafts also decline, and occupational specialists return to rural pursuits. During this process, the old forms of labor conscription, such as bondage and slavery, give way to new methods of controlling the subordinate classes under local military fiefs. Feudal regressions of this type followed all civilizational expansions prior to the emergence of the Mercantile Revolution. The latter, which was succeeded almost immediately by the Industrial Revolution, caused progressive changes in human societies of such an intensity that feudal regressions occurred only in exceptional societies. Some of the latter remained economically marginal only for short periods, while others had a social structure that was too rigid to permit technological renovation and the corresponding social reorganization.

Actually, human history records more regressive steps of the various kinds just reviewed than steps forward. In spite of their prevalence, however, regressions are only temporary setbacks stemming from an exhaustion of the potentialities of a productive system or of a particular form of social organization. By contrast, evolutionary steps are cultural renovations which, once achieved and dispersed, permanently enlarge the human capacity to produce and consume energy, to create increasingly inclusive forms of social organization, and to achieve ever more reliable conceptualizations of the external world.

In summary, sociocultural evolution is viewed here in two ways: (1) as a series of evolutionary stages expressed in a sequence of sociocultural formations, each generated by the action of a cultural revolution via one of its civilizational processes, and (2) as an interplay between cultural progressions and regressions, and between historical incorporations and evolutionary accelerations. This conceptualization replaces the prevailing and much criticized view of evolution as a sequence of fixed and necessary stages (either unilinear or multilinear) with a broader and more varied perspective; it envisages evolution as a dialectic movement in which both progress and regression are necessary constituents. This view also implies that each technological revolution will follow a different history in a new context from that of its original context. Thus a great variety in expression is to be expected since (1) change is more often brought about by diffusion than it is generated internally; (2) diffusion does not make available to receiving societies all the elements originally developed, nor are these elements acquired in their original order or with the same associated elements; (3) the civilizational processes are propelled by technological revolutions that give an advantage to the groups that first experience them, permitting their expansion as centers of domination; and (4) peoples influenced by the same civilizational process through historical incorporation, lose command of their destiny and are reduced to a state of subjugation and dependency that severely limits their possibilities for subsequent development.

In addition, the point of view adopted here provides for the conceptual integration of the various individual civilization processes corresponding to divergent lines of multilinear evolution into a global process, which is the historical reality. This permits an evaluation of both positive and negative aspects of the interaction between the individual processes. It also permits generalized reconstruction of the relationships between modern peoples throughout the world and the civilizational processes that have shaped the great cultural traditions within which their present cultures have been crystallized. Finally, this viewpoint makes possible the erection of a typology of technological revolutions, civilizational processes, and sociocultural formations that is applicable to the classification both of past societies at varying levels of development and of contemporary societies with differing degrees of complexity.

Archaic
Societies

The Agricultural Revolution

The first civilizational process stems from the Agricultural Revolution, which began some 10,000 years ago among the peoples of Mesopotamia, Anatolia, Palestine, and Egypt, and which was later repeated, as a result of diffusion or independent development, in India (6000 B.C.), China (5000 B.C.), Europe (4500 B.C.), tropical Africa (3000 B.C.), and the Americas (2500 B.C.). This technological revolution equates with two civilizational processes, one leading to agriculture and the other to pastoralism. It created ways of life so sharply differentiated from those of earlier times that the two new sociocultural formations are recognizable from their earliest appearance. Crystallization of the first process resulted in the Undifferentiated Horticultural Villages (not stratified into classes), whose people practiced root or cereal cultivation. Some later combined agriculture with animal raising, but they did not employ their animals for traction. The second process brought about Nomadic Pastoral Hordes, which specialized in animal breeding and whose total way of life was adjusted to the conditions favorable for the survival and reproduction of the herds.

Prior to the Agricultural Revolution, men lived in small migratory bands as hunters, fishermen, and collectors of roots and fruits. Their existence was rigidly controlled by the rhythm of the seasons, and oscillated between feast and famine. Only in exceptionally favorable regions, as on sea coasts rich in shellfish, were larger population concentrations possible. Even here, group size was limited by the food supply during lean seasons, and by the absence of social mechanisms for maintaining solidarity among larger groups. During this long pre-agricultural period, estimated to have endured some half a million years, man learned to control fire and to make tools. Both abilities compensated for his lack of biological weapons for attack or defense and increased his food-getting efficiency. He developed languages and created social institutions to regulate family and group life and to intensify sentiments of ethnic loyalty. He also accumulated a heritage of knowledge and belief that explained his experiences, guided his behavior, and assured his emotional stability in the face of the uncertainties of life and his growing awareness of the existence of pain and death.

The basic characteristic of pre-agricultural human groups was their multiplicity and diversity. Each small band, living in isolation and subdividing if it grew too large, developed a distinctive outlook and viewed other bands with hostility. The centrifugal forces that prevailed under these circumstances led to a dispersion of the human species from its original habitat to the ends of the earth. It also led to adaptation to the most varied ecological conditions by diversification and specialization of the initial generalized cultural tradition. Institutions like the incest taboo and the practice of exogamy created bonds between social groups, combining them into cooperative or at least non-hostile tribal units. The linkages that resulted from these institutions facilitated the diffusion of cultural advances, making it possible to capitalize on the creativity of larger numbers of people and to accumulate a growing body of common knowledge. To judge from the ethnological data, this interfertilization was enhanced by other practices, such as wife stealing, which must have played an important role in the diffusion of certain kinds of technology.

As a result of man's accumulation of observations and experiments over the millennia, the first agricultural practices appeared in some of these groups. They took the form of tending fruits and roots in tropical areas, and of the cultivation of cereals in temperate or cool regions, all of which had formerly been gathered as wild plants. Such practices gradually led to a new productive process, one making it possible to reorganize nature and place it at the service of mankind (Vavilov, 1926; Sauer, 1952; Curwen and Hatt, 1953). Animal domestication, which appeared in certain areas, enriched the human diet with a regular supply of meat and milk, as well as making hides readily available. Later on, domesticated animals provided a new source of muscular energy for transportation (riding) or for pulling plows or wagons, greatly enlarging both the productive capacity and the spatial mobility of mankind.

Like agriculture, animal domestication probably developed gradually from a series of accidental occurrences that familiarized man with the conditions required for survival and reproduction of animals. According to ethnographic evidence, hunters like to bring home to their wives and children the young of animals they hunt, to be raised as living playthings.

Such acts may have led to domestication, first of hunting dogs, then of birds, swine, and many other dooryard animals, and finally of larger herd animals such as reindeer, camels, sheep, horses, and cattle. Ultimately, pastoralism emerged as a specialized way of life.

It may be postulated that pastoralism arose independently of agriculture as a result of corralling the excess animals obtained from hunting or by a process parallel to that followed by some American Indians for the re-domestication of horses and cattle, which were introduced by Europeans, escaped captivity, and multiplied astronomically in wild herds on the vast natural pastures of the New World. The absence of archeological evidence in the Old World for this hypothesis makes it seem more likely that pastoralism developed from the domestication of animals by farming groups at the level of Undifferentiated Horticultural Villages. The tending of animals in appropriate places, distant from the fields, could have led to increasing occupational specialization and to functional, occupational, and finally ethnic differentiation between horticulturists and pastoralists. Whatever the exact way, the result was gradual bifurcation of the most advanced human groups into two markedly different lines of development.

From the standpoint of man's relation to nature, the most significant result of agriculture and pastoralism was the enormous demographic growth made possible by the increased food supply. This demographic explosion was expressed in two ways: initially, in fission and lateral expansion, which constituted the dynamic factor of the Agricultural Revolution; and subsequently, in agglutination and vertical stratification, which became more marked in the succeeding Urban Revolution. The former tendency stems from inability of the social system to prevent subdivision of a group whose population exceeds certain limits, or to unify numerous small and scattered nuclei into a single ethnic entity. While the new productive techniques were capable of enlarging the size of each nucleus, they did not yet permit man to be completely sedentary or to create large social units of extra-familiar composition. Consequently, the earliest groups of planters and herders were obliged to lead a mobile existence by the continuous need for virgin land for their fields and new pastures for their herds, and to subdivide into new ethnic units as their populations increased.

As the vanguard of a new technology, tribal groups of agricultural and pastoral peoples spread over large areas, displacing the indigenous populations whenever they occupied land suitable for crops or herds. In this way, increasingly extensive agricultural and pastoral areas, fringed by marginal groups, developed in different parts of the world. As time passed, the hunters and gatherers were reduced to small enclaves, which continued their ancient way of life, having been left behind by history. Ultimately, most of them were gradually affected by the civilizational process originating from the Agricultural Revolution and integrated into an agricultural or pastoral economy.

Undifferentiated Horticultural Villages and Nomadic Pastoral Hordes

Societies falling into the category of Undifferentiated Horticultural Villages or Nomadic Pastoral Hordes were primarily dedicated to subsistence pursuits. Nevertheless, disputes with each other and conflicts with less advanced peoples whose land they appropriated led to the rise of warfare as a major occupation. Ethnic units began to ally themselves periodically with other local groups or with independent hordes for joint attack or defense, providing a basis for the emergence of larger ethnic units. Under these circumstances, the purely usufruct relation that prevailed between pre-agricultural bands and their territories was modified. Although the institution of land ownership had not yet developed, tribal units became joint tenants of lands improved by human labor or of pastures needed for their herds and assumed collective responsibility for their preservation in order to insure group survival and autonomy.

Like their hunting and gathering predecessors, these incipient agricultural and pastoral economies did not yet provide conditions for internal socio-economic diversification. All members devoted themselves to subsistence activities and were differentiated only by family lines, sex, and age. Collective exploitation of hunting, fishing, and gathering resources was extended to farming and herding lands, permitting each family to remain a unit of production and consumption. Both private accumulation of goods and private appropriation of the fruits of labor were unknown. Surpluses were distributed in ceremonies or during festive social gatherings. Even when such goods were appropriated by the heads of family groups, they generally reverted to the community after death or were redistributed according to classificatory kinship rules, making them available to most if not all members of the local group.

In these two formations, various kinds of social organization based on classificatory kinship systems were adopted to satisfy the requirements for an institutional response to a growing productive capacity. Both bilineal and unilineal kinship systems—the former associated with different kinds of family organization, and the latter tending toward clan structure—can be amplified to deal with more inclusive ethnic units. Because of this, attempts to correlate classificatory kinship models with progressive forms of sociocultural development are doomed to failure. This is a sector in which the number of possible responses to innovations in the productive system is so great that the results, although not arbitrary, are difficult to utilize for construction of evolutionary sequences (Murdock, 1949; Levi-Strauss 1949, 1953).

The most significant institutional innovation at this stage probably was a strengthening of sexual division of labor by alloting to women the tasks related to the planting, harvesting, and preparation of cultivated foods. This new responsibility continued traditional patterns, in the sense that it gave women the more routine tasks and men the more arduous ones. Thus, where men formerly hunted, they now became responsible for clearing forests and preparing the land for planting. Both are exacting tasks, but their episodic nature leaves long periods for rest and the renewal of strength. Women's work, on the other hand, included new daily tasks like housekeeping, food gathering and preparation, and child care, all of which require continuous efforts without time for relaxation. Simultaneously with this differentiation of productive roles, beliefs and rites began to develop in order to bolster the social preeminence of men, whose dominant status was no longer justified by the predominance of the male role in the subsistence economy.

This status problem did not arise among Nomadic Pastoral Hordes because male activities remained preeminent in subsistence. On the contrary, male dominance was strengthened into despotic patriarchal forms. In groups of mixed economy, in which herding was men's work, men also retained their social dominance. Warfare was another factor that fortified male supremacy in agricultural and pastoral societies and led at an early time to the appearance of social distinctions. Old forms of chiefdom were amplified as a result of increased responsibilities issuing from the need to deal with threats to crops and herds and to fight for new agricultural and pasture land. Concurrently, the number of religious specialists was enlarged in order to handle more complex functions, such as assuring the fertility of soils and seeds or the health and multiplication of herds.

During the course of the Agricultural Revolution, some societies significantly augmented their productive capacity by replacing the hoe with the animal-drawn plow and by using fertilizers. Technology was further enriched by the discovery and dissemination of pottery, which facilitated the cooking of vegetable foods. Spinning and weaving also developed, permitting cloth to replace leather garments. These activities devolved principally on women and added to the hardship of their daily routine. Men spent less time hunting and fishing and more in agriculture and animal care. As a result, each person's sphere of circulation became increasingly restricted, and sedentary tendencies were correspondingly augmented.

This new technology could not yet support either full-time specialists or social stratification into economic classes. Classificatory kinship continued to be the principal mechanism of social organization, and family groups and local communities remained both the operative units and the focus of group loyalties. Everyone was a food producer, and only the most elementary forms of exchange existed for products or services. Within each local community, newcomers acquired the same rights as older members and, by the process of learning the language, became heirs of a common cultural tradition. Membership in the group gave access to community lands and herds, and entailed the obligation to participate in collective efforts at providing the conditions necessary to insure the survival and expansion of the society. Each individual possessed the same knowledge as all the rest, devoted himself to the same task—except for the already specialized roles of chiefs and priests—and lived in a restricted social world where all adults were acquaintances and equals.

THE URBAN REVOLUTION

As the Agricultural Revolution progressed, the accumulation of technological innovations brought some societies to the level of a new revolution and to an evolutionary acceleration that resulted in the creation of new sociocultural formations. The mechanism was the accumulation of new techniques that progressively enhanced the productive capacity of human labor and brought about alterations in institutions related to production and distribution. As a result either of diffusion or of independent invention, or a combination of the two, this transformation took place in various parts of the world, in different ecological conditions, and in different cultural contexts. The number of cultivated plants was increased and their genetic character perfected. Agricultural technology was revolutionized by the adoption of more efficient methods and tools for preparation of the soil, and for the transport and storage of crops. Certain societies with a pastoral or mixed economy achieved similar advances through genetic selection in their herds and specialized breeding of animals for riding and traction or for the production of meat, milk, and wool.

The most important technological innovation at this stage was irrigation, which made it possible to control one of the most crucial factors in agricultural production and consequently to assure increasingly abundant harvests. In low lands, this was accomplished by control of natural river flooding, and at higher elevations by construction of complex systems for the capture and distribution of water through artificial canals. Other basic innovations included general use of the plow and wheeled vehicles, both of which employ animal traction, and of sailing vessels able to undertake coastal navigation. Generally, these systems of traction and transportation appear together in the Old World; in the New World, however, the absence of large domesticated animals led to different lines of development.

By employing different combinations of these technological innovations, certain peoples revolutionized their food-producing capacity, providing the basis for the rise of the first cities. New industries appeared, among them the manufacture of tiles, bricks, and glass, and copper and bronze metallurgy; ideographic writing, seals, numeration, the calendar, and monumental architecture were more widely disseminated. Childe (1946) has shown that these technological developments were concentrated within a relatively brief period of two millennia preceding 3000 B.C.; consequently they tend to assume an explosive character that contrasts with the low rate of creativity prior to that time. Societies in the forefront of this technological revolution increased the productive capacity of each worker sufficiently to free growing numbers of people from subsistence activities. More complex forms of division of labor, based on craft or commercial specialization, began to develop both within and between communities.

Elaboration of these tendencies led to occupational stratification and this in turn transformed the internal structure of society. The lateral expansion that for millennia had multiplied the number of independent groups now began to be offset by a new vertical orientation, which permitted both the growth of individual ethnic groups and their fusion into increasingly larger entities. The processes of social stratification and political organization that came into being were accompanied by mechanisms for compelling greater productivity and for the accumulation and concentration of wealth by minority groups, whose defense of their special privileges acted as a further stimulus to economic development. During this process, the productive system became increasingly complex and consequently required more intensive exploitation of resources for its maintenance. Simultaneously, there developed new ways of ordering ethnic units, which permitted greater internal differentiation through segmentation into opposed but mutually complementary social strata. Growth took place both by internal population expansion and by the incorporation of peoples with different ethnic origins. In some such societies, prisoners of war were no longer ceremonially sacrificed, but instead were exploited as captive labor, leading to the emergence of slavery. The presence of slaves, who represented human beings depersonalized into instruments of production, profoundly affected the way of life of these societies; they ceased to be egalitarian, and were transformed into multi-ethnic communities in which slaves contrasted with their lords and entered into competition with the free laborers.

The basic impetus for this social differentiation came from technological renovation, which made it necessary to regularize the distribution of surplus goods within the community, to increase power of compulsion over other groups, and to organize the internal social life of ever more populous human communities. Relatively few alternative organizational possibilities existed. One was private property in land and slaves; another, the preservation of universal access to the land combined with new forms of political and religious organization that provided incentives for increased productivity and the accumulation of wealth. The technical progress achieved by societies that adopted an intensive agricultural economy made the challenge to develop effective social utilization even more imperative. At a certain point, its confrontation led to the appearance of occupational specialization and more elaborate methods for exchange of goods and services. It also led to the regulation of the labor force and a progressive differentiation among individuals according to their role in production. This gave rise to social classes in which producers were differentiated from the parasitic levels that appropriated the surpluses. The latter were concentrated in the emerging cities, where they served as tax collectors, or as middlemen between the already distinct groups of farmers and herders, or between these and the artisans. As craft specialization grew, artisans increasingly tended to abandon subsistence activities and to congregate in the cities.

In some societies, the concept of private property, which was originally restricted to the fruits of labor of each individual or family, was progressively extended until it became a primary factor in social life. Ultimately it embraced the agents of production, draft animals, enslaved workers, and even the essential of agricultural production, the land. In this way, the possibilities for accumulation of property were increased, and wealth not only became concentrated in the hands of a few and was conspicuously consumed, but it also became an instrument for the production of additional wealth. In other societies, by contrast, the collective form of property was preserved, generally in association with newly developed techniques like irrigation and with the creation of extra-familial institutions for regulation of productive activities and integration of craftsmen and agriculturalists into self-sufficient communities. In such cases, the social structure was able to evolve toward higher forms of communalism, which allowed ethnic expansion and sociocultural progress without employing the devices of private property and personal enslavement of the workers.

All these avenues led to the creation of forms of social interdependence that transcend simple family solidarity and local mutual aid. New threads of interdependence began to regulate the interchange between different sectors of the society: between food producers on the one hand and the specialized craftsmen and various parasitic groups concerned with social regulation on the other. Two types of societies took shape, one dominated by privatistic principles, especially private property and slave labor, and the other based on collective ownership of the land and non-enslavement of the labor force. These distinct lines, which gave rise to distinct sociocultural formations, must be classified into two civilizational processes. The latter corresponds to the transition from Undifferentiated Horticultural Villages to Rural Craftsman States of the Collectivistic type, while the former corresponds to Rural Craftsman States of the Privatistic type, either derived by internal evolution from horticultural villages or the product of their subjugation by Nomadic Pastoral Hordes. Both kinds of Rural Craftsman States emerge when the egalitarian condition of primitive kinship-regulated societies is superseded by the state with a new type of social organization that is based on civil ties and social stratification. Morgan (1877), who emphasized this transmutation, called the old form "societas" and the new one "civitas." Simultaneously, a third civilizational process took place in some regions, by which certain Nomadic Pastoral Hordes specialized in the breeding and training of animals for riding and warfare advanced under the influence of bronze technology to become Nomadic Pastoral Chiefdoms.

In Rural Craftsman States of the Privatistic type, slavery assumed a personal stamp and gained increasing impetus. It stimulated wars of conquest for expansion of territorial domain and conversion of conquered populations into personal slaves, who initially were impressed into the agricultural labor force and later increasingly into manufacturing and transportation activities. This new composition of the labor force affected both the subjugated peoples, who were uprooted and converted into a "necessity of life" for other groups—comparable to cattle or a natural resource—and the subjugators, on whom new ways of life were also imposed. This new dynamic factor influenced all later social development. Relations between lords and slaves assumed a character of domination unattainable with any other type of goods, and this character permeated the social structure. As a consequence, the sociability, equality, and homogeneity of earlier times were gradually replaced by stratification, in which some members of the society were specially privileged and others were reduced to outcasts. With the expansion of both servile classes and groups freed from the necessity of manual labor, a special mode of life arose, sustained by new values that emphasized wealth and power rather than strength and accomplishment. Little by little, this process brought into existence a nobility that tended to control not only the slaves but the whole society, the better to preserve and enhance its own privileged status.

In both types of Rural Craftsman State, the transformation of villages into towns and cities resulted in progressively greater differentiation of the peasantry, until it ultimately became a distinct social stratum. Indeed, the peasantry as a social category appears with the emergence of urban life (Redfield and Singer, 1954). Henceforth, the rural and urban components of society, although always interrelated, became increasingly differentiated into separate cultural traditions with distinct ways of life. In this new rural-urban social dichotomy, descent was replaced by territory as the basis for social unity, permitting the incorporation into a single sociopolitical unit of diverse local communities with large populations of varying origins and unlike ethnic composition, as well as differing degrees of social stratification.

One of the main challenges confronting these early stratified societies was the development of integrative principles able to give social unity and moral cohesion to populations divided into strongly differentiated and conflicting social strata, and to weld them into unified and operable political entities. A major source of cohesion was encountered in ancient religious traditions, which could be redefined so as to console the poor for their poverty, to minimize their envy of the rich, and to permit everyone not only to live and interact, but to find beauty and significance in their contrasting forms of existence. Specialists in dealing with the supernatural grew in importance and became part of the ruling class. Their numbers included not only learned men who explained human destiny, but also technicians who directed the labor force and determined the appropriate times for different kinds of agricultural activity. Later on, these specialists collected and codified traditional knowledge, adapting it to new requirements but in so doing tending to congeal it for all time. Such conservatism was inevitable since their status as guardians of revealed truths was dependent upon divine authority and power, and rules made by the gods cannot be modified without risking loss of faith.

During this process, the shamans or medicine men were converted into priests. To fulfill their new functions, the priests organized into bureaucratic bodies of growing size, and temples institutionalized what had formerly been community religious observances. These institutions soon became the primary agencies of social organization, and operated from ceremonial centers of increasing magnificence, whose construction and maintenance had two crucial effects: (1) By requiring appropriation of increasing amounts of goods and services, they supplied the sacred motive necessary to induce the peasantry to produce more than it could consume, thus providing an external direction to the productive process. (2) The need to recruit temporary labor for the erection of temples provided a mechanism for the disengagement of increasing numbers of workers from the villages to form an urban labor force. From this force, the most talented artisans were selected for the manufacture of jewelry, ornaments, and luxury articles for the cult or other special uses. Thus government, which had previously been a matter of traditional leadership, came to be the function of a separate bureaucratic class, in which precedence was taken by new figures who fused together political and religious power by becoming living gods.

Rural Craftsman States and Nomadic Pastoral Chiefdoms

There are two basic models of Rural Craftsman States, which reflect distinct civilizational processes. The Collectivistic model corresponds to the city-states that initiated fully urban life based on irrigation agriculture and collectivistic socio-economic systems before 4000 B.C. in Mesopotamia (Halaf), between 4000 and 3000 B.C. in Egypt (Memphis, Thebes), around 2800 B.C. in India (Mohenjo-daro), and before 2000 B.C. in China (Yang-Shao, Hsia). The same level of development was attained much later in other parts of the Old World, such as in Transcaucasia (Urartu, 1000 B.C.), southern Arabia (Hajar Bin Humeid, 1000 B.C.), Indochina (Khmer, 500 B.C.; Champa, A.D. 700; Annam, A.D. 1000; Siam, A.D. 1200), and Indonesia (Xrividjava, A.D. 750; Madjapahit, A.D. 1293). In the New World, examples are provided in the Central Andes (Salinar and Gallinazo, 700 B.C.; Mochica, 200 B.C.), in Mesoamerica (Uxmal, A.D. 300), and in Colombia (Chibcha, A.D. 1000). Japan is exemplified by Jimmu (at the beginning of the Christian Era), Heian (A.D. 782), and Kamakura (A.D. 1200).

The second model is represented by Rural Craftsman States of the Privatistic type, and is exemplified by the first mature maritime states, such as the Phoenicians (Tyre, Sidon, and Byblos, between 3000 and 1000 B.C.), the Minoans (Knossos, 1700 B.C.), the Mycenaeans (1700 B.C.), the Etruscans (9th century B.C.), Athenians (6th century B.C.), and Romans (before the 3rd century B.C.). Other examples are Israel (1000 B.C.), the trading states of Central Asia (Kushan, 500 B.C.), and Russia (Kiev and Novgorod, A.D. 1000). Of somewhat doubtful character are the so-called African "kingdoms" apparently based on slavery, like Ghana (9th century A.D.), Zimbabwe (10th century A.D.), Mali (13th century A.D.), Gao (14th century A.D.), Congo (15th century A.D.), and Songaye (16th century A.D.). Their delayed maturation permitted these African formations to adopt a series of technological developments originating in other areas, such as metallurgy, and to imbue themselves with values emanating from the great cultural traditions. As a result, their Rural Craftsman State structure assumed a distinctive form.

The third civilizational process released by the Urban Revolution corresponds to the expansion of the archaic pastoral formations, and gave rise to the Nomadic Pastoral Chiefdoms. Examples are provided by "desert people" like the Hyksos, Hittites, and Kassites (1750 to 1500 B.C.), who fell upon the Egyptian and Mesopotamian civilizations; by the Aryans (1300 B.C.), Scythians (500 B.C.), Huns (A.D. 200), and Sakas (120 B.C.), who advanced in successive waves over the oriental civilizations; by Teutonic, Celtic, and Viking warriors, who attacked Roman civilization after the 3rd century; and by the Arabs, Berbers (A.D. 600), Tartars, Mongols (A.D. 1200), and Manchus (A.D. 1500). Some of the latter were of sufficiently late development to incorporate iron technology, and this propelled them rapidly through the operation of another civilizational process into a new type of sociocultural formation, the Despotic Salvationist Empires.

The Urban Revolution, acting through the three civilizational processes that issued from it, not only created the rural-urban dichotomy, but also produced two divergent forms of rural life: the peasant and the pastoral. Although in many instances individuality was retained, providing a basis for continuing cultural diversification, three general life styles can be easily recognized. Because they constitute adaptations to specialized social and environmental conditions, they took a similar form in urban, peasant, and pastoral populations the world over, regardless of linguistic and cultural diversity.

Both types of Rural Craftsman States came into being with the appearance of supra-community political units in the form of cities that exerted domination over a more numerous rural population (representing 80–90 percent of the total state population). This rural contingent was either dispersed over the surrounding landscape or concentrated in peasant villages, where it maintained its centuries-old way of life untouched by the radical changes underway in the cities. Family units and kin-based solidarity continued to be the principal mechanisms of social integration. Existence remained routine and varied only with the changing seasons, each of which brought a repetition of the previous year's activities. Men and women worked successively in agriculture, animal breeding, and household indus-

tries. There was little room for specialization since everyone knew all the
basic productive techniques, although these were practiced along sex and
age lines. Nor was there opportunity for open competition, or for novelty
or innovation. A deep feeling prevailed that life was unchanging, that
traditional knowledge incorporated all that there was to be known, and
that earthly goods were limited. A deep-rooted hostility developed toward
city populations, based on the notion that urban residents were incapable
of doing real work, and that they lived by exploitation of the peasants,
and were consequently responsible for the latter's misfortunes, including
wars and pestilences (Redfield 1953; Foster 1962, 1965).

In the emerging cities, the future style of life was beginning to take
shape. It was characterized by ambition and expansionistic ardor, and was
supported by a body of explicit knowledge developed in an atmosphere
permitting some degree of cultivation of an inquisitive spirit. Greater social mobility stimulated competition for control of the sources of wealth,
power, and prestige, all of which were now defined more objectively and
treated more opportunistically and aggressively. Some centers came to
specialize in robbery or piracy. As they grew stronger, they became dominant over or developed commercial relations with large populations, whose
surpluses they absorbed. Some reached a high level of development and
played a dynamic role in the evolutionary process comparable to that of
pastoral formations, by implementing cultural diffusion through commerce and warfare.

The Nomadic Pastoral Chiefdoms, limited by the requirements of
their wandering herds, never became sedentary, and consequently never
developed beyond incipient social stratification and differentiation. Their
more homogeneous society, and smaller and more isolated population units, as well as their fluctuating work schedule—in which periods of great exertion alternated with long periods of recuperation—were
not compatible with rigid stratification. The mobility provided by the
horse and camel was combined with an adventurous spirit to imprint upon
these pastoral peoples a special life style and qualities of agressiveness and
pride that made them not just different from but completely opposite to the
peasantry. Maturation of these features transformed the Hordes, and later
the Nomadic Pastoral Chiefdoms, into the terror of the rural population,
which was unable to defend itself against attack. Consequently, the rural
population was frequently obliged either to pay tribute or to suffer periodic

raids, and ultimately to succumb to political domination by the pastoral chiefs.

Pastoral formations of this kind developed on the periphery of the Rural Craftsman States. They served as specialized sources of oxen for pulling plows and carts, of donkeys for carrying burdens, and of horses and camels for riding and warfare. Archeological evidence shows that by the beginning of the second millennium B.C. some pastoral groups already possessed the metallurgical technology necessary to manufacture horse bridles and other types of harness. More efficiently equipped for warfare, they began to fall, first upon rural populations, which they modified ethnically and socially, and later upon the centers of urban civilization themselves.

As can be seen, the Urban Revolution not only accentuated differences between the agricultural and pastoral ways of life, but also placed them in marked opposition to one another. The interaction between these two conflicting formations played a dynamic role of primary importance in the subsequent evolution of human societies. The zeal for expansion and conquest manifested by pastoral peoples forced many agricultural societies to develop into Rural Craftsman States, whose organization afforded superior possibilities for defense against attack. This had two major effects: (1) Multi-ethnic societies were formed in which political ties were strengthened at the expense of kinship and tribal ones; and national units were created that were capable of imperialistic expansion by the subjugation and incorporation of disparate populations into extensive economic and political systems. (2) Privatistic types of society were favored by the fact that collective ownership and universal access to land by farmers was incompatible with the needs of the herders and also by the practice of awarding parcels of land or groups of people as bounty to the conquerors.

The structure of the Rural Craftsman States resulted from the simultaneous operation and constant interaction of two aspects of the social order. One was the regulation of economic life by institutionalization of property as an incentive to the production of surplus and by monopolization of this surplus by a minority class. The other was the institutionalization of political power in the form of the State. The best examples of Rural Craftsman States based on private property and slavery are provided by the maritime states, which developed to exploit the potentialities of commerce and warfare, and which tended to become multi-ethnic entities with a rigid class structure. Their populations were divided into free men, whose social condition varied according to their wealth in goods, slaves, and lands; and a large subordinate stratum of slaves, which included both war captives and formerly free citizens who had lost their means of livelihood.

Development of the Privatistic type of Rural Craftsman State was more a consequence of external conditions than of an internal evolutionary process. In fact, its existence was dependent upon the prior maturation of other societies with which trade could be conducted. A minimum of internal development was an indispensable prerequisite, however, to specialization in commercial or manufacturing activities, or to such undertakings as large-scale shipbuilding, which required both a wide variety of raw materials and the kind of organized effort possible only under centralized authority at a supra-community level. Power increased along with wealth, in part because the ships engaged in commerce also conducted wars of defense and offense, and also because of the emergence of the first slavistic colonial systems, which placed large bodies of people in other countries at the service of the ruling classes. This combination of commercial, military, and colonial activity permitted early Privatistic societies to become increasingly powerful, and ultimately to destroy the centers of civilization that originally catalyzed their existence.

In the most advanced Privatistic societies, the upper class succeeded in appropriating not only foreign territory, but also the lands of its own peasantry, thereby reducing the latter to a labor force alienated from its own interests and subjected to an external will. Since the object of this domination was acquisition of the benefits of surplus production, consumption by the workers tended to be severely restricted. Thus, under forms of social organization conducive to the increased production of goods, a realization of the potentialities in the new technology led to the impoverishment of a growing proportion of the national population, as well as of foreign slaves. And what was more important, this poverty did not stem from natural obstacles or rudimentary technology, but from the social concomitants of production; that is, from the constrictive power of the privileged class. In some societies, the process of stratification was extended until the entire population was divided into a dominant minority, composed of the owners of the land, cattle, and instruments of labor, and a dependent majority, which formed a free or enslaved subordinate class.

The Collectivistic type of Rural Craftsman State was based primarily on irrigation agriculture and state ownership of land. Both of these were controlled by a central authority of a religious character, which supported itself by levies of tribute and labor rather than by personal enslavement of the labor force. Although states of this kind are also prone to wars of conquest in order to enlarge their domain, they differ from the Privatistic type in not being dependent on warfare as a permanent source of the slaves required to maintain the productive system. Furthermore, their ruling classes develop by an elaboration of the traditional criteria of leadership and consequently tend to show a higher level of social responsibility toward their peasant and craftsman populations than is exhibited by the rulers of Privatistic states.

During the initial period of development, the organization for production in Collectivistic states continued tribal lines of cooperation (Steward, 1955). Later, these tended to be replaced by increasingly rigid forms of labor conscription by the State and its bureaucracy, which grew in size and power as the irrigation systems were expanded. Political authority also grew increasingly despotic as ever more ambitious projects were undertaken, both in irrigation, which strengthened the economic system, and in monumental architecture, which weakened it.

Since the economic structure of Collectivistic formations does not provide the upper classes with a competitive incentive, stagnation may occur. Counteracting this tendency, however, are mechanisms to stimulate productivity and foster reinvestment of surplus goods. Conspicuous consumption by those in charge of public functions, and the exercise of political power by high religious and bureaucratic hierarchies as well as by military leaders, encourage the production of luxury goods, the construction of residences, and the wider use of services, although at the cost of increasing sacrifice on the part of the dispossessed classes. In some instances, exploitation of the masses became so oppressive that it provoked peasant insurrections, such as occurred in Egypt in the 22nd century B.C. In spite of this potential threat however, the fact that the primary dynamic mechanism of Collectivistic states is provided by disputes over power rather than by the acquisition of personal wealth from productive or commercial activities, gives these states greater social and political stability than those of the Privatistic type.

Another basic innovation of the Rural Craftsman State was institutionalization of incipient systems of government into a state type of organization. This occurred in response to three major imperatives: (1) the need to pre-

serve group solidarity and the capacity for self-defense in internally differentiated societies, in which the destiny of each person was fundamentally
linked with that of his class rather than to the State; 2) the requirement
for maintenance of internal order which in non-egalitarian societies can be
achieved only by the creation of special bodies for social control and repression; and (3) the necessity of delegating to central organs responsibility for
the planning, execution, and control of services of collective concern, such
as construction and maintenance of irrigation networks and many other
services of increasing complexity and urgency.

The primary institutions in the Rural Craftsman States reflect the form
of property regulation that prevails. In the Privatistic type, economic exploitation was based on private property and slavery; in Collectivistic societies, it was controlled by institutionalization of the technico-bureaucratic
functions resulting from state ownership of land. Both types of state must
fulfill similar general functions, among them preservation of order, render-
ing of services, administration and procurement of resources, and above all
formal regulation of social life. Codification of social norms was accomplished in Collectivistic states by the priests, who undertook to adapt traditional ways to the new requirements of a more diversified social life. The
resulting legal-religious statutes established the non-egalitarian social order
as a sacred order, whose commandments and rules were enforced throughout
the domain. These codices contain explicit statements of the general objectives of the society, the attainment of which is the personal responsibility of
every citizen. They specify correct behavior for the individual, along with
rewards for conformity and punishments for abuses. They also define
recommended or prohibited activities as well as the rights of the individual.
In short, they establish the general rules within which social life and competition between the different strata of society should proceed.

Formalized by the state structure, the emerging non-egalitarian social
order produced extremes of wealth and poverty, of despotic power and
oppression. Tribal equality and family or clan fraternity were replaced by a
new kind of solidarity, the civic tie, and a new criterion of social quality,
that of stratification. The former imposed the language, customs, institutions,
and beliefs of the dominant ethnic group on all those peoples incorporated
within the orbit of state domination, destroying their former traditions in
order to integrate them into the state society at the bottom of the cultural
and institutional hierarchy. The latter, namely social stratification, made

class membership more important to the destiny of the individual than either family situation or tribal affiliation.

Exercise of the functions of maintenance of internal social order, external defense, and the promotion of ethnic expansion required that the State progressively enlarge its services of administration, social control, repression, and warfare. To defray rising costs, it was obliged to levy tributes that consumed ever greater portions of the production, and simultaneously channeled increasing numbers of people into nonproductive activities like warfare, public construction, and bureaucratic tasks. Concomitantly, the State began to assume functions formerly exercised by other agencies. Justice ceased to be a private family or clan matter and became the concern of specialists. Maintenance of order became the duty of state police. Finally, warfare, which had formerly been the obligation of all adult males, became the pursuit of specialized leaders and permanent troops, which could be mobilized not only against external enemies but also against internal threats of revolt by the subordinate classes. This was an inevitable development in Rural Craftsman States of both types because the sedentariness of the peasants and the specialization of the artisans made them increasingly unfit for warfare, and so left the society vulnerable to assault by Nomadic Pastoral Chiefdoms. Incorporation of permanent military commanders into the state power structure, however, became one of the principal sources of internal agitation, because of the ambitions stimulated by the existence of an autonomous military power with the capacity to seize the machinery of state.

The major external functions of the State are defense and warfare. The former is essential to preserve its territorial dominion and the autonomy and liberty of its citizens; the latter is the instrument for expansion over other groups. The State also guarantees the stable and orderly conditions indispensable for commerce. Although trading practices existed at the tribal level, the transport of large volumes of goods requires conditions of security and of peaceful coexistence that are possible only under the aegis of authorities respected by all.

The development of institutions for the maintenance of internal order in the earliest Rural Craftsman States was thus prerequisite to emergence of mercantile societies based on pastoral or maritime activities. The first nuclei of Minoan or Mycenaean civilization which, along with Phoenicia, played a crucial role in the diffusion of the progress achieved in Mesopotamia and Egypt, actually were extensions of other civilizations. However, the merchants did not play a totally passive role. In many cases, they promoted the initiation of commercial relations by offering the opportunity for trade as an alternative to pillage. Especially along seacoasts, the trader became a displaced intercultural agent. As an intermediary between productive sectors in his own society, he had long occupied a parasitic and somewhat alienated position; his new role simply made him more marginal than before. As a result he could transfer his loyalty from an ethnic or cultural group to whoever guaranteed his freedom to trade and to prosper.

In societies where state ownership of property prevails, the objective of the State is to maintain a social order composed of free and equal proprietors, all of whom share the obligation to cultivate the lands and to produce manufactured goods so as to create a surplus that is available to the State in the form of tribute. Nevertheless, the existence of a political center external to the communities over which it exercises directive functions, and of distinct bodies of tribute collectors, warriors, and priests, tends to break down the egalitarian social structure. The State, in the form of a permanent central government integrating the whole society, imposes a dominant minority over the bulk of the population, which assumes the role of subjects. The emergence of this minority, which is called upon to exercise a regulatory role and is able to compel obedience through its monopoly of the legitimate instruments of coercion, caused the breakdown of family, clan, and tribal autonomy. The dominant group was initially composed of individuals whose prestige came from leadership in warfare or other traditional sources. With the passage of time, however, membership tended to become self-perpetuating and its privileges were enhanced by inheritance and by education. Under these circumstances, the ruling class changed from a neutral power to one that favored vested interests. As a consequence, states of the Collectivistic type also develop a clearly defined power structure composed of a hereditary nobility, military chiefs, religious leaders, and high bureaucrats. Although united by their common antagonism to the mass of the population, these factions are in eternal conflict with one another over the most advantageous form of social order.

Once in existence, such states tend toward increasing regimentation of social activities in the effort to perpetuate the interests of the dominant groups. Counteracting this tendency, however, are deeper forces that originate from the dynamics of opposition between the diversified social categories and, more importantly, from the technological innovations that expand the sources of wealth and power. These pervade the social order and hinder its solidification by continually forcing a redistribution among the various sectors within the ruling class of the fruits of labor and of opportunities for exercise of power and the enjoyment of social prestige.

Rural Craftsman States of the Collectivistic type have a theocratic structure with a strong tendency toward centralization, and are ruled by traditional monarchies. Concentrated in the person of the king are nominal ownership of the land, the highest religious authority (often involving personification of the divinity by the ruler), supreme command in warfare, and the direction of the bureaucratic machine. The most influential and highly differentiated social groups within this structure are the nobility, priesthood, military leaders, and bureaucrats. All these categories tend to become hereditary, with the result that they develop into privileged castes. Concomitantly, the peasantry and craftsmen also assume a hereditary character.

With the passage of time both Privatistic and Collectivistic types of State take on a militaristic configuration as a result of emergence to predominance of the military hierarchy, which imposes itself despotically over both its own people and the subdued foreign populations. The Spartans constitute an extreme example of this model, developed on the basis of a slave economy. Other examples include states resulting from the conquest of agricultural societies by pastoral chiefdoms, such as the Hyksos domination of Egypt, the Kassite and Hittite states of Mesopotamia, various subjugated regions in India, and the successive dynasties of Mongol rulers in China.

A third configuration, of even later development, is exemplified by democratically organized city-states like those of the Greeks and early Romans. These Privatistic societies offered greater opportunity for upward social mobility to both merchants and the rural oligarchy, thus broadening the ruling stratum and leading to development of democratic institutions. Although controlled by a patrician group, this political structure is distinct from centralized church-state and militaristic types of governments, and replaces hereditary criteria with more egalitarian and competitive procedures for recruiting members of the ruling class. These more democratic structures never achieve the stability of the other types, however, because of the opposition between interests of free citizen-proprietors, the lower class (which is also free but never equal), and the slaves (neither free nor equal). The reconciliation of these interests requires the creation of formal institutions for social control, which leads inevitably to repression, to the fortification of militaristic tendencies, and to the emergence of dictatorial regimes. The most typical features of such political systems are the absence of priestly domination and caste differences, and the presence of a middle class within the urban population; all these provide wider opportunities for intellectual speculation and debate, and establish conditions under which scholars and artists are free to exercise their creativity.

All these kinds of political organization significantly affect social progress because they subordinate all activities to the objectives of the groups in power. The expansion of productivity, permitted by continuing technological advances that stemmed from the Urban Revolution, came under the control of vested interests whose primary concern was to keep the rich rich, and the poor poor. Incentives for technological change were minimized in Collectivistic states by the availability of large masses of labor in a condition of servitude, and in Privatistic states by the abundant supply of slaves obtained in warfare. As a result, progress was much slower during the two millennia following 3000 B.C. than it had been during the two millennia preceding that date.

Paradoxically, therefore, although the Urban Revolution held the potential for greater freedom from want, most of humanity that came under its influence was condemned to extremes of slavery or servitude previously unknown. This occurred because its diffusion did not take place by the free adoption of technological discoveries, but through the domination and force exerted by the first societies to acquire the new technology and to experience its renovative effects. The various civilizational processes spawned by the Urban Revolution were able to consolidate the myriad of microethnos, each of which possessed its own language and culture, into a smaller number of entities equating with larger political units. These developed into expansionistic states and entered into conflict with one another, giving rise to new national ethnic bodies which, in turn, projected their influence, language, and customs, as well as a new productive technology, over increasingly extensive areas. At a certain stage of expansion, such an enlarged ethnos became vulnerable to attack by its subjugated populace, which had assimilated the new technology during the process of domination and had matured sufficiently to reassert independence. There followed the "dark ages" or proto-feudalism, during which commercial relations and bonds of sovereignty were interrupted. Each population then undertook the reconstruction of its own ethnos until one was able to dominate the others, thus initiating a new cycle of expansion, or until the emergence of a new civilizational process interfered by generating one or more new sociocultural formations.

During the ten millennia since the beginning of the Agricultural Revolution, and the 6000 years since the inception of the Urban Revolution, all the peoples of the world have been affected. Even marginal groups that have resisted integration into the new ways of life have suffered profound influence.

Regional
Civilizations

The Irrigation Revolution

In spite of its immense potentialities, the Urban Revolution led only to the creation of successions of local feuding states. These were still expanding when another technological revolution began and crystallized a new formation that was capable of inaugurating the first regional civilizations. This was the Irrigation Revolution, which provided the technological foundation for the Theocratic Irrigation Empires that arose in Mesopotamia with the Akkad Empire (2350 B.C.) and the Babylonian Empire (1800 B.C.); in Egypt with the Middle Kingdom (2070 B.C.) and the New Kingdom (1750 B.C.); in India with the Maurya Empire (327 B.C.) and the Gupta Empire (A.D. 320); in China with the Chou (1122 B.C.), Chin and Han (220 B.C.), Tang (A.D. 618), Ming (A.D. 1368), and Ching (A.D. 1644) dynasties; and in Indochina with the Cambodian Empire (A.D. 600). Later, in the Americas, the Maya[1] (A.D. 300), Aztec, and Inca Empires developed, which were still in existence at the time of the Spanish Conquest. Japan also emerged into civilization (Tokugawa, A.D. 1603) via a Theocratic Irrigation formation inspired by the Chinese model.

Technological, institutional, and ideological ingredients that had been accumulating for a long time in Rural Craftsman States of the Collectivistic type came into full flower with irrigation agriculture employing complex canal systems operated from urban centers, which later became metropolises heading extensive networks of cities. Some of these civilizational processes developed independently, as appears to have occurred in Mesopotamia and the Americas; others may have been stimulated by the adop-

---

[1] The Maya, like the Khmer, have been classified as Theocratic Irrigation Empires because they most closely resemble this formation, although neither developed irrigation agriculture because of environmental conditions in the tropical areas where they flowered. This tropical forest setting provided wood and other perishable materials for house construction, resulting in an extreme contrast between the majestic ceremonial centers and the "poverty" of the habitation zones, where simple dwellings have left little archeological trace.

tion of technological and institutional innovations originally made else-where. Whichever the case, the resulting sociocultural formations are so radically different from earlier and later ones that they can only be under-stood as distinct entities produced by the maturation of a new technological revolution, namely the Irrigation Revolution.

These new civilizations were founded on technical discoveries and insti-tutional innovations that followed the appearance of sedentary agricultural communities and social stratification. The most important advances were made in irrigation and fertilization which, under the management of centralized governments, brought a pronounced increase in agricultural productivity and a corresponding enlargement of the food surplus. This not only stimulated population growth, but freed large groups of peo-ple from subsistence activities for other tasks, which ranged from the con-struction of impressive tombs and the extensive hydraulic works required for large-scale irrigation, to wars of conquest. Other significant advances in-cluded the expansion of copper and bronze objects and of pottery to general use; the invention of tiles, new construction techniques and materials, and new mechanical devices (like the pulley, press, and windlass); and the further development of ideographic writing and numerical notation. These innovations combined with other elements to cause an evolutionary ac-celeration in some societies that led to revolutionary advances; in other societies, profound reflexive modifications were produced via historical incorporation.

The increased demand for indispensable raw materials, especially min-erals, led the Theocratic Irrigation Empires to improve their land and water transportation, and to engage in warfare and commerce, all of which expanded and strengthened external ties. Manufactured goods were stand-ardized, and some items began to be produced for commercial ends. Where metallurgy was best developed, wars were fought with metal weapons and with battle chariots possessing reinforced wheels. Expansion of trade created a need for more precise standards of exchange, and thus led to the appear-ance of metal coinage in some areas.

Theocratic Irrigation Empires

This new formation is characterized by a highly centralized state organiza-tion that tightly integrates all sources of social compulsion and eliminates any interests likely to offer opposition. Such a concentration of strength was achieved by the consolidation of military, political, and religious control, and by the monopolization of productive and commercial activities. As a consequence, these formations do not contain either independent churches or private enterprises that might compete with the central power. Such monolithic control permitted the Theocratic Irrigation Empires to broaden their internal economic base by a major expansion of their irrigation systems; to stimulate the growth of cities through urbanization programs and the construction of aqueducts, dikes, and ports; and to build gigantic temples, palaces, and tombs, as well as extensive road networks, monumental defensive walls, and enormous navigation canals.

The economic basis for these large undertakings was provided by appropriation of the cultivatable lands by the theocratic state and by development of complex administrative measures to control the labor force. Appropriation was accomplished by vesting nominal ownership of all land in the Pharoah, the Inca, or his equivalent, who had become a living deity. This allowed the state to intervene in the work routine of the peasantry, to control hereditary succession in such a way as to increase productivity, and to establish regular procedures for the collection, storage, and distribution of surpluses. Under this system, agricultural land remained under the management of local communities without an intermediary property owner, but the self-sufficiency of the peasant villages was destroyed by their integration into a larger economic system.

Administrative controls were strengthened by the creation of a vast priestly bureaucracy for regulation and supervision of the labor force. The scope and technical complexity of state enterprises made it necessary for this bureaucracy to become specialized and to some extent secularized in order to recruit the personnel required to plan and direct engineering works, to introduce uniform systems of weights and measures, to administer taxation, to survey and allocate cultivated lands, to collect and distribute food, to develop accounting procedures for recording supplies of goods and labor, to regulate external commerce for the acquisition of raw materials like minerals, wood, and salt, and to establish educational institutions for the formal transmission of both traditional and techno-scientific knowledge.

This organizational development manifested itself in the appearance of a vast body of state servants to supplement the hereditary nobility and the priests, who had originally performed these tasks. Although initially selected on the basis of ability, these new public servants also tended to form a restricted and inbred social circle because of two factors: (1) the necessity for formal training to carry out their duties, and (2) the fear of dilution of their rights and privileges. As a result, sons began to inherit their fathers' posts, and the bureaucracy was gradually transformed into a caste with growing affinities to the nobility and priesthood, and increasing alienation from the bulk of the population.

Another organizational feature of the Theocratic Irrigation Empires was professionalization of the army. This was made necessary by the unsuitability of the peasantry for combat and by the vulnerability of the complex irrigation systems to external attack. Later, these professional military bodies occupied themselves not only with defense against invasion or insurrection, but with wars of conquest. Even when recruited from the ruling class, military men tended to view themselves as members of a new and independent entity, with the result that they first vied for control of newly conquered regions and later challenged the authority of the central government. The fact that their power structure was not sanctioned by traditional religious sources, but depended on simple force, also made military groups intrinsically subversive. Their presence imbued the great centers of civilization with a lust for pillage of the kind that formerly pervaded only marginal pastoral and maritime societies, with the result that the expansionism of these rich societies was no longer motivated by a desire to enlarge the productive base, but rather by the need to satisfy the ambitions of a functionally differentiated class for power, wealth, and prestige. This expansionism aggravated tensions within the ruling class and caused internal economic problems that were reflected in increased despotism.

In some instances, militaristic expansion appears in response to internal demographic pressures resulting from the inadequacy of resources to supply the needs of a growing population. More frequently, however, militarism is a consequence of the subjugation of civilized peoples by more warlike societies, whose members then dominate the ruling class (Steward, 1955). This seems to have happened to the Theocratic Irrigation Empires of Mesopotamia and to the Aztec Empire, both of which were marked by extreme militarism. When theocratic power gives way to militarism or becomes allied with it, despotism tends to increase because a war economy demands greater sacrifices from all members of the society. Under such conditions, the ruling classes lose their sense of social responsibility, which formerly assured not only to the peasant but even to the captive a degree of autonomy that almost resembled freedom in comparison to subsequent forms of personal enslavement of the labor force by individual owners.

In the Theocratic Irrigation Empires, the peasant remained coupled with the land and was obliged to suffer expropriation of his surplus production. Above him and regulating his life was the community in which he lived, and beyond this was a royal bureaucracy that was personified by the agents who collected tribute or taxes, and who conscripted labor. These forms of appropriation could be justified, however, since they were not for the enrichment of the nobility, but primarily for the support of basic public services. The luxuries enjoyed by the dominant class were provided from what was left over, and were a form of compensation to the nobility, priests, military chiefs, and bureaucrats for the services they rendered to the central government. Even when he was conscripted for construction of massive structures like temples and pyramids, the peasant or the artisan was contributing to the perpetuation of values, beliefs, and splendors that were as meaningful to him as to his masters. Captives brought from distant lands to labor on these projects were permitted to live together, to raise their children, to preserve their language, and to continue those customs that were compatible with the new life. The captivity of the Jews in Egypt shows that these enslaved masses were not introduced into the system as the property of individual masters, but rather as defeated peoples subjugated to the state, which had the power to free them at any time or move them to new lands. This distinction is important because it facilitated the ethnic integration of conquered groups into the peasantry or into the bodies of artisans and soldiers of the imperial macro-ethnos. Captives put to work in mines or on the construction of Cyclopean buildings suffered a more despotic form of subjugation, although even their condition remained distinct from that of slaves.

The recruitment of large masses of people for productive activities was facilitated by the special character of the state-church, which was polarized around a divine monarch, who granted to the clergy an extraordinary number of social, political, and economic functions, and whose acts were sanctioned by the most transcendental values. As spokesmen for a sacred regency, the priests could compel the working masses to produce surpluses, to pay tribute, and to contribute their labor for great public undertakings with more effectiveness than could have been attained by any other kind of authority.

The Egyptian temples provide extreme examples of this regulatory system. One in existence at the time of Ramses III (12th century B.C.) operated as a vast financial and administrative enterprise over an enormous productive area. It controlled 750,000 acres of cultivatable land, 107,000 captive workers, 500,000 head of cattle, a fleet of 88 ships, and 53 factories and shipyards (White, 1959, p. 326). In addition to this economic role, the temple exercised other general functions, among them the regulation of social life by the establishment of rules of conduct that affected every individual. It prescribed and performed the rites that marked the passage of life from birth to death and beyond, and it created and executed the calendar of religious observances and productive activities. It also directed the educational institutions that trained priests and members of the other ruling classes. This coupling of its role as intermediary between the living and the supernatural with its economic and regulatory functions created an extraordinary degree of power for compulsion and discipline. Fused with the state, it constituted a monolithic and all-powerful political entity.

A serious drawback to this form of social organization is its expense. Maintenance of a large and parasitic priestly corps, and the erection of elaborate temples, and especially the construction of royal tombs, absorbed the greater part of the surplus that could be produced. It has been estimated that construction of the pyramid of Cheops occupied 100,000 workers for some 20 years. Supplying them with even minimal amounts of food and clothing must have consumed the surplus production of about three million peasants, considering the level of development of Egyptian technology at that time.

As we have seen, the Rural Craftsman States had already produced cities, which were differentiated from the predominantly peasant villages by their function as centers of political, administrative, religious, military, and commercial activity. With the advent of the Theocratic Irrigation Empires, some of these cities became the political capitals of expanding empires. This transformed them into the nuclei of extensive urban networks that occupied large territories, and into centers of cultural creativity and of diffusion of great cultural traditions. Their populations increased and diversified, both occupationally by the development of functional specializations, and ethnically by the incorporation of people with different origins. Other traditional functions also acquired new dimensions as these cities developed into great imperial and commercial centers that integrated large areas, from which raw materials and artifacts were obtained and to which money and manufactures were exported. They also served as sources of the diffusion of a more advanced technology and a more formalized cultural tradition.

In these great cosmopolitan metropolises, the intellectuals (typically composed of priests) emerged as a new ingredient in the social order with the capacity to develop a body of explicit knowledge distinct from the orally transmitted learning of the common man. The activities of this new class led to the invention of writing, mathematics, and astronomy, and to the application of scientific knowledge to productive technology, monumental architecture, and metallurgy—first of copper and bronze and, later, of iron. Metal tools, initially restricted to swords, plowshares, and wheel and axle hardware, were diversified to include implements for the manufacture or construction of a wide variety of products that ranged from pyramids, temples, palaces, and houses to ships and mills.

Some urban civilizations based on irrigation agriculture endured for millennia, making them the most stable sociocultural formations known to history. Their ability to persist for long periods, through cycles of ascendency and decadence, resulted from the structure of their social stratification, which contained few sources of internal dissention. The high degree of integration and centralization achieved by their sociopolitical institutions also assured a strong social cohesion and organic solidarity.

Two disruptive tendencies can be recognized, however. First, the economic burden inflicted by the vast parasitic class tended to increase in weight with the accumulation of special prerogatives in the form of land cessions and labor pools, with the restriction of certain types of economic activity (especially trade) to particular individuals, and the increasing costs of temple and pyramid construction. Second, the development of militarism not only strengthened a social component that was capable of imposing its hegemony on other sectors of society, but also tended to deform the economic system by permitting the expansion of imperial power over areas that could not be incorporated into the irrigation technology, but were coveted instead for their mineral wealth or their ability to provide captive workers or tribute. Both of these tendencies led the Theocratic Irrigation societies to decadence by undermining the foundations of their social structure. Bureaucratic deterioration characterized societies of this type in Peru, India, and China, and reconstitution of the economy began to take place in those regions along Privatistic lines. The militaristic tendency was most pronounced in Mesopotamia and developed to a lesser extent in Mexico, but it has manifested itself to some degree in all Theocratic Irrigation Empires, with a resultant weakening of solidarity and decreasing ability to withstand assault by marginal populations.

Because of these disruptive tendencies, the monolithic irrigation formations always fell into feudal regressions on reaching a certain level of development. Other factors contributing to this result were exhaustion of the potentiality of the irrigation technology by over-exploitation of the land, the absence of a stimulus for technological innovation because of the existence of an unlimited labor supply, and the suppression of intellectual curiosity under the weight of religious traditions. The latter situation reduced the intelligentsia to mere custodians of sacred knowledge, who were rarely capable of creativity. These factors manifested themselves initially in disputes within the dominant classes and in civil wars, and ultimately in vulnerability of the Empire to external attack, which led to centuries of regression or stagnation until restorative forces once more gained ascendency.

While external attacks are a constant ingredient in all cases of collapse of imperial, irrigation-based structures, they probably served only to aggravate an already deteriorated situation resulting from internal dysfunctions and the loss of macro-ethnic integration. Deprived of many institutions conducive to social solidarity and impressed into an increasingly despotic system of production, the lower classes ceased to identify with their rulers and became increasingly susceptible to surrender to external attack with little or no resistance. This passive attitude represented a form of combat, or at least protest, by the subordinate classes against the oppression to which they were subjected. This process can be observed in Egyptian civilization, which was prostrated initially by the Hyksos, under whose rule resurgence was achieved. Later, during the New Empire, attack by the Sea Peoples, Lybians, and Nubians forced the whole region into a feudal regression from which it never recovered. The irrigation civilizations of Mesopotamia had an even more agitated history, marked by successive attacks from the Aryans, Kassites, Hittites, Sythians and, finally, the Medes and Persians. Restorations followed several of these defeats and subsequent dips into feudalism; although each new foreign regime produced profound changes in ethnic composition, similar technological and structural principles were maintained until a new civilizational process swept over Mesopotamia.

The irrigation civilizations in India were attacked by the Aryans, Sakas, and Huns, and a variety of other Mongoloid-Tartar groups, and plunged into successive periods of feudalism. They emerged several times but ultimately fell into a long period of feudal stagnation, which lasted until the peoples of the Indus and the Ganges were revived by subsequent invasions and incorporated into new civilizational processes. The first of these was the Iranian invasion, which created the Sultanate of Delhi; the next was the Tartar, which imposed the Timurid regency; added together, these totaled nearly six centuries of foreign domination. Finally came the British, who subjugated India for a century and a half through the colonial process of historical incorporation, and who led the Indian population into the underdeveloped status that characterizes it today.

Chinese civilizations were also exposed to constant pressure from neighboring groups, especially the Eurasian pastoralists, to whose chiefdoms they were four times subordinated. The first domination was by the Ch'tan barbarians, who imposed the Liao dynasty. Later, attack by the Jurchen introduced the Chin Dynasty. This was followed by the Mongols, who established the Yuan dynasty. Finally, the Manchu invasion created a new and final dynasty. Each of these invasions led to a period of feudalization during which the invaders became acculturated as a preliminary to the slow process of imperial restoration. Because of its capacity for acculturation, China alone of all the Theocratic Irrigation Empires (and of past high civilizations in general), has been able not only to survive but to maintain its macro-ethnic structure basically intact. Its most recent experiments, like the popular communes and the cultural revolution, to a large degree represent restorations of ancient social institutions and reconfrontations of the threat of bureaucratic despotism that has been faced unsuccessfully for millennia. The irrigation civilizations of the Americas never suffered disruptions of equal magnitude, with the exception of the Chichimec invasions of highland Mexico, but all were ultimately destroyed by the Spanish Salvationistic Mercantile expansion.

Assertions about the supposedly static and despotic character of civilizations based on irrigation stem principally from observation of these societies after they have plunged into feudalism. Marx (1904, 1965), for example, characterized such formations as essentially stagnant on the basis of the situation in India and China during the 19th century. Wittfogel (1955, 1957) has been able to depict them as intrinsically despotic only by including in the category of "Asiatic societies" many formations that have nothing in common with civilizations based on irrigation. Such characterizations do not hold up (1) when the social vigor and cultural creativity of the Theocratic Irrigation Empires at the climax of maturation of their developmental potentialities is taken into consideration; (2) when it is recognized that the alternative method of regulating the labor force at that level of sociocultural evolution was personal slavery combined with private ownership of land, which was far more despotic; (3) when it is admitted that, like all civilizations, they were subject to periods of decline into feudalism with loss of macro-ethnic integration, political unity, and economic vitality, not because of conditions that are attributable to any of the formations from which they emerged, but because this is an intrinsic characteristic of feudalization; and above all, (4) when other conceptual categories are employed for the classification of truly despotic formations, none of which is either based primarily on irrigation or traceable to such an origin.

THE METALLURGICAL REVOLUTION

Expansion of the Theocratic Irrigation Empires was limited by the inapplicability of irrigation to some conquered areas because of different ecological conditions. Where irrigation could be introduced, the basic technology could be implanted by programs of colonization employing populations already incorporated into the dominant ethnic group. Where irrigation was not feasible, only weak domination could be exercised. In spite of this drawback, however, the technology developed by the Theocratic Irrigation Empires diffused over extensive areas, revolutionizing the way of life of innumerable people. The impact was so profound and the renovations were so radical that it seems necessary to us to view this expansion as a new technological revolution, the Metallurgical Revolution which, in turn, was responsible for the appearance of a new sociocultural formation, the Mercantile Slavistic Empires.

The improved technological base consisted principally of the generalization and perfection of iron forging for the manufacture of tools, weapons, plowshares, wheels and axles, and metal ship parts. Other significant elaborations included coinage, improved vehicles for transportation and warfare, merchant and fighting ships, and phonetic writing and decimal numeration, all of which had existed in rudimentary form in previous formations. To these were added hydraulic engines, water-powered mills, aqueducts, rotary millstones, derricks and windlasses, and lighthouses.

Mercantile Slavistic Empires

The Mercantile Slavistic Empires, having developed from Rural Craftsman States of the Privatistic type, are characterized by the institutionalization of private property in land, by the stimulation of commercial freedom, and by the expansion of efforts to obtain war prisoners for sale into slavery. Mature examples of this formation include the civilizations of Assyria (12–17th century B.C.), Achaemenia (6–4th centuries B.C.), Greece (5–1st century B.C.), Carthage (6–2nd centuries B.C.), Rome (27 B.C. to 4th century A.D.), and Byzantium (6–10th centuries A.D.). Although they exhibit marked differences, which stem from their preceding cultural traditions and the unique historical vicissitudes they experienced, all these civilizations are variations of the same sociocultural formation, based on enslavement of the majority of the labor force and the fostering of mercantile colonialism.

These civilizations possessed either a locally developed or a borrowed technology, and contrasted structurally with empires based on irrigation. Because of the general availability of the ore and the simplicity of the conversion process, iron-working techniques could be diffused without limitation, permitting widespread use of metal tools. These made it possible to clear forests and to place under cultivation extensive regions whose lower productivity per unit area was compensated for by an almost unlimited extension. Dissemination was further facilitated by the perfection of sailing ships and wagons or carts. Phonetic writing promoted literacy, which had been previously restricted to the priesthood, with a resulting increase in all types of knowledge. Coinage made possible a monetary economy, and this in turn greatly expanded the horizons of foreign trade. Together, these developments created a freer type of society that stimulated individual achievement and provided enterprising persons with ample opportunities for enrichment.

This civilizational process derived its major impetus from the mercantile economy, which linked hundreds of communities by sea or land, bringing to each the internal modifications necessary to advance them from production for subsistence to production for trade. In the principal cities of each Mercantile Slavistic Empire, there was a proliferation of craft shops organized like *ergasterions*,[2] and encompassing a wide range of craftsmen, including carpenters, cabinetmakers, boatbuilders, metalworkers, coppersmiths, brickmakers, potters, glassblowers, tanners, jewelry makers, saddlemakers, leatherworkers, and shoemakers. In such institutions tens or even hundreds of craftsmen, the majority of them slaves, produced standardized articles for sale.

The potentialities of the Mercantile Slavistic formation received only incipient expression in the Assyrian and Achaemenian civilizations. A more advanced stage was achieved by Greek civilization, by the colonial expansion of Carthage, and especially by the Roman Empire. These latter empires had their origin in the expansion and multiplication of city-states that were ruled by rich merchants, and which later became structured into vast systems unified by warfare and integrated by trade. After a long period of maturation as cities exerting dominance over the surrounding rural area, during which they were characterized by equality within their patrician class, the city-states turned to the establishment of colonies in Europe and Africa. Here a concentration of slave labor obtained through warfare permitted the development of plantations and *ergasterions* for the production of food and goods for export. In this way, an international market was created, which was further stimulated by the simultaneous development of a monetary economy and erudite culture in various cities. Disputes between the city-states over territorial boundaries opened the door for the establishment of the Mercantile Slavistic Empires.

The Mercantile Slavistic character of the new economic system led to more radical forms of social order and carried to extreme lengths the waging of wars both for conquest and for the capture of slaves to augment the labor force. At the same time, the monetary economy intensified internal

---

[2] *Ergasterion* is the Greek word for workshops or "factories." The *ergasterions* were rudimentary forerunners of modern factories and were created for the "industrial" production of certain types of goods by occupational specialists, in some instances with the aid of mechanical equipment like pottery wheels, rotary mills with animal traction, hydraulic wheels, hammers, etc. Demosthenes, the celebrated Attic orator, was also known as the proprieter of two *ergasterions,* one employing 20 slaves for the production of furniture, and the other utilizing 32 slaves for the manufacture of shields (Childe, 1946).

competition for wealth. In Athens and Rome, four-fifths of the population was composed of slaves and even higher concentrations existed in the colonies around the Mediterranean.

Generalization of these economic procedures destroyed the last surviving forms of communal property (*ager publicus*) and the remaining institutions based on kinship relations. Classificatory kinship (in which collateral and lineal relatives are called by the same terms, thus creating large groups with close solidarity) was transformed into descriptive kinship, which employs special terms to distinguish lineal relatives and, in so doing, reduces the boundaries of family solidarity and restricts inheritance. Subsequent steps toward the rationalization of conduct included the secularization of a number of aspects formerly under religious control, and the individualization of social relations. Usury became institutionalized, and the concept of a land mortgage was created, which led to the practice of enslavement for debt. Inheritance was legalized through wills. Ultimately, the entrepreneur emerged supreme in every sector, with the capacity to subordinate even the power of the State to his interests.

The wealthy minority became increasingly powerful and the subordinate masses, whether free or enslaved, ever more miserable, thus heightening social tensions to an extreme degree. It became legal for a citizen to sell himself or his children, and this occurred frequently in periods of hardship. It also became common practice to sentence debtors to temporary servitude, especially during periods of warfare. Simultaneously, emancipated slaves were able to grow rich through commercial speculation and to enter the nobility, establishing wealth rather than birth as the primary criterion of social status. Citizenship, which had originally made all patricians co-governors of their city and individually responsible for the just conduct of social and political life, became diluted and lost its significance. Roman citizenship, once limited to descendants of the ancient lineages, became generalized over the whole non-servile class. Simultaneously, social tensions and disputes between city-states were intensified. In reacting against such threats, both Greece and Rome moved toward super-statism and dictatorial regimes. These measures were in vain, however, because each system had reached the climax of its potentiality, and had generated irreconcilable contradictions that caused it to plunge inevitably into feudal regression.

The flexibility of their entrepreneurs, the nearly universal applicability of their basic technology, and the strength of their compulsive power over the labor force, made the Mercantile Slavistic Empires far more dynamic centers of cultural diffusion than the Theocratic Irrigation Empires had been. Colonization of near and distant peoples was followed by their incorporation into civilization, and in some cases by their cultural and linguistic assimilation as sub-varieties of the imperial macro-ethnos. The foreign slaves were acculturated as a result of their concentration in metropolitan centers and their incorporation into the productive system, but in this process the ethnic composition of the native population was modified and social tensions were developed that ultimately destroyed the viability of the system. By dispersing their productive and military technology over wide regions via commerce and warfare, these Empires accelerated the maturation of other ethnos, arousing in them ambitions for plunder to which the conquerors themselves ultimately fell victim. Maturation of the aspirations for freedom among some of the conquered groups led to the outbreak of insurrections that animated the slaves and the "external proletariat," and created conditions favoring the reconstitution of ethnos capable of self-government.

As a consequence of this process, the climax of the Roman Empire, like that of many other Mercantile Slavistic Empires, coincided with its point of maximum weakness, representing as it did a macro-ethnos within and outside of which were evolving ever more cohesive and vigorous ethnic nuclei. When the attacks of subjugated peoples against the imperial center were added to slave rebellions, destruction of the Empire became inevitable. The whole complex consequently deteriorated, fragmenting into a multiplicity of feudal components and eradicating a large part of the technical and cultural progress that had been achieved.

Certain Nomadic Pastoral Chiefdoms also played a significant role in the decline of the Mercantile Slavistic Empires. Because of special cultural and ecological circumstances, they were able to become producers and consumers of metal objects without adopting sedentary agricultural life. Under these conditions, they not only retained their ancient warlike proclivity, but even intensified their audacity and combativeness. These ethnically cohesive, extra-imperial peoples were irresistibly attracted by the accumulated wealth of their neighbors, and gave the coup-de-grace to the Mercantile Slavistic formation. The latter had exhausted its vitality and had dichotomized into ruling classes weakened by comfort and luxury, and masses of slaves and peasants in revolt against their despotic subjugation.

The loss of bonds integrating these dominant and subordinate classes contributed to the defenselessness of the society. The same passivity that had existed among the dependent strata in the irrigation formations (which were also unable to mobilize for defense against invasion) developed here, and constituted a form of non-violent protest against the prevailing despotism. Unable themselves to subvert the system, the lower classes must have viewed disruption of the oligarchical domination by warfare as offering a better prospect than perpetuation of existing conditions.

In Europe, Roman sovereignty crumbled before an audacious handful of barbarians who, though numbering less than half a million, devastated, defeated, and subdued 80 to 100 million Romanized Europeans and Africans. These barbarians, who could contribute little to the civilization of the peoples they dominated, infiltrated what remained of the old formation. Their chiefs became the aristocracy and royalty of the imperial provinces, while their warriors turned into sedentary peasants or formed new contingents of artisans. Whatever their rank, the majority learned the Roman language and all adopted Roman culture.

As this analysis has shown, both Theocratic Irrigation formations and Mercantile Slavistic ones die out without initiating a new civilizational process. They simply sink into feudal stagnation, fragmented into innumerable, small, local potentates that are incapable of mercantile production or foreign commerce. Reduced to subsistence activities, they are condemned to ineffectual gestures of defense against external attack. In both formations, the macro-ethnos derives its vulnerability from its imperialistic expansion, which brings more peoples under its jurisdiction than can be acculturated and assimilated. The concomitant loss of ethnic cohesion by the original imperial nucleus and destruction of its political unity brings to an end its existence as a civilization.

In all feudal contexts regardless of origin, the former slaves are first converted into *colonus*, who pay rent for use of the land, and who ultimately amalgamate with the free farmers to constitute the feudal peasantry. This transition from slavery to servitude comes about less often as a consequence of the struggle of slaves against their masters than it does by evolutionary deterioration of an economic system in which slaves once played a fundamental role in the production of commercial goods. Under conditions of feudal stagnation, where the cities fell under the domination of rural potentates and where most of the economy became localized and self-sufficient, this transition made little difference to the nobility. The slaves, however, who had produced the goods for sale and who in return had been fed and clothed, became converted into serfs bound to the land and required not only to pay tribute in goods or services, but also to feed and clothe themselves.

The post-Romanic feudalization of Europe resulted from two deep ruptures. The first developed in the imperial authority system, which broke down into thousands of fiefs that were incapable of amalgamating into a durable political structure. The second occurred in the mercantile system of exchange, which survived only as a marginal, semi-clandestine activity on the part of those who traded with Arabs, Jews, and Syrians. Once the mercantile activity and political unity were destroyed, other regressions took place, among them the reversion of agricultural estates to communal or church control. Slave-produced manufactured goods were replaced by household industries conducted by the women of each family. As a result, craftsmanship, which had been urbanized and disassociated from agriculture, was re-amalgamated with the rural subsistence economy. Only very slowly were crafts resumed in the decadent cities, leading to the appearance of guilds, which tended to be monopolistic and to promote the hereditary transmission of professional skills.

The major consequence of all these regressions was a solidification of social stratification, which replaced the formerly high social mobility. At the summit was the nobility, composed of blood descendants of the barbarian invaders now transformed into feudal proprietors. Next in line were their most prominent servants, the clergy and the vassals, from whose numbers were recruited bodies of cavaliers who were more concerned with sporting contests than involved in warfare. Beneath these was the urban population, composed mainly of small merchants and craftsmen, the latter divided into masters, skilled artisans, and apprentices, all of whom were segmented into guilds and concerned with production for local barter. At the base of the social pyramid were the peasants, who were bound to the soil either as serfs or tenants.

This feudal world settled into peaceful stagnation, disturbed only by invasions like that of the Moors, by religious wars, or by disputes between nobles. The ancient Roman civilization dissipated into a mere tradition, following the pattern manifested earlier by the decline into feudalism of the Theocratic Irrigation Empires. The only integrating force was provided by a religion inherited from one of the component groups of the former empire, which redefined tribal concepts to make them more broadly applicable. This minority religion—which provided consolation for the afflicted, which recognized no ethnic privileges or social gradations, and which was able to show men a destiny beyond mere existence—became the heir of the Greco-Roman world, just as other Asiatic minority religions like Buddhism, Confucianism, and Hinduism attained dominance over other feudalized contexts. This religious re-integration could not restore the ancient empires, however, except periodically and weakly. Nor could it prevent subjugated but still viable ethnic groups from combining their ancient traditions with those introduced by the barbarian invaders to produce new ethno-national configurations.

The Roman Church slowly achieved a monopoly over economic life by appropriating the small available surplus through tithes, bequests, and gifts; and redistributing it in "political charity"; and by directing the construction of cathedrals which, along with castles, comprise the only significant architectural creations of the Middle Ages. Its wealth grew unceasingly as a consequence of the monopolization of lands and herds, the progressive enlargement of fields controlled by the abbeys, the administrative control of the only construction projects where employment could be obtained, and the general rapacity displayed by its monasteries and religious orders. Concomitantly, the Church became a great regulating force in social life, where the egalitarianism of primitive Christianity had given way to rigid social stratification, conformism, discipline, and obedience.

Post-Romanic feudalism, like other feudal societies, brought an amelioration of despotism because it broke down the political and economic integration of large areas. Peasant communities probably were able to eat, dress, and live better than they could under the grip of the empires, whose authoritarian structure had permitted the commandeering of all surplus goods and the conscription of persons. In the cities, whose populations were drastically reduced, the artisans found ways to develop a cooperative organization that was less vulnerable to swindle and abuse than the earlier Greco-Roman *ergasterions*. Although liberation from the conscriptive power of powerful economic and political-religious structures of the past did not lead either the peasants or the artisans to launch significant exploits, it did permit a tranquil existence, if one lacking in grandeur.

Absence of a central authority with the power to enforce social regulations also opened the door to pillage and highway banditry. Such activities became the means of livelihood for multitudes of ruffians, who were protected by feudal lords for whom they presented opportunities for increased wealth. Above all, society and culture sank into increasing mediocrity, with a resulting incapability for intellectual creativity and technical progress. In such surroundings, only theology flourished, having dedicated itself to the compilation of varying sources of learning and speculation about revealed truth.

The Pastoral Revolution

During the technological revolutions thus far examined, several civilizational processes have succeeded one another. The Urban Revolution unleashed the impulses responsible for the advent of two divergent models of Rural Craftsman States, and for advancement of the Hordes to Nomadic Pastoral Chiefdoms. With the Irrigation Revolution, the Theocratic Irrigation Empires were crystallized. In response to the Metallurgical Revolution, the Mercantile Slavistic Empires arose. Each of these civilizational processes advanced and retreated in different regions and at different times, catalyzing the lives of thousands of people, raising some to the level of high civilizations and incorporating others into spheres of foreign domination. During the course of each individual process, various civilizations arose, lived out their destiny, fell, and plunged into feudal regression. From the ruins, new civilizations grew, introducing new variations, but based on the same general technology and structured along similar lines. Such was their resistance to fundamental alterations that even when devastated by attackers, these civilizations were generally able ultimately to absorb, assimilate, and acculturate their aggressors, and to re-establish their basic forms of cultural expression.

It was only under the impetus of a new civilizational process stemming from a new technological revolution that another type of civilization could be achieved, which represented a new stage of cultural evolution and a new sociocultural formation. This is what happened when the maturation of the Pastoral Revolution provided culturally retarded peoples with a new military technology that permitted them to attack the feudalized areas of high civilizations, to resist assimilation by them, and to create a sociocultural formation totally distinct from previous ones—that of the Despotic Salvationist Empires.

This new civilizational process originated during a new wave of pastoral expansion that was stimulated by application of products of iron technology to the cavalry. The most diagnostic elements include the saddle provided with stirrups, which gave the rider greater security and mobility; the metal shoe, which extended the useful life of animals and made it possible to employ them on all kinds of terrain; and the iron bit manipulated by reins, which increased the rider's control. Later additions included improved methods of harnessing draft animals, which permitted more efficient exploitation of their strength and eliminated the suffocating effects of the neck collar. Other technical innovations also diffused at this time were new types of wind and water mills, which were first used to pump water, grind grain, and press oil from seeds, and later to crush ore and to drive saws, bellows, and other mechanical devices. Of these new elements, those that revolutionized the cavalry and armed the warriors with more efficient swords and lances were responsible for the onset of expansionism, while the ones most crucial to the establishment of new sociocultural formations were the more efficient exploitation of animal energy for agriculture and transportation, and the harnessing of the energy of winds and water for the service of man.

The earliest of these technological innovations had a vitalizing effect on the older Nomadic Pastoral Chiefdoms, leading them into confrontations with more highly developed societies. Formerly, the consequence had been to plunge the latter into feudalism, and to transform the invaders into new aristocracies that simply repeated the older forms. Now, however, when feudalized areas were attacked, they were reawakened culturally and integrated into a formation totally distinct from all previous ones. This was the Despotic Salvationist Empire, structured along new regulatory principles in which the dominant role was played by a body of messianic religious beliefs. These beliefs did not serve either as an integrating force between conflicting social strata or as a means of social regulation, but instead channeled the energy of whole populations into the sacred mission of imposing on the world the divine truth that had been revealed to them. Naturally, economic interests allied themselves to this divine mission.

The military cavalry technology and new ideological armor transformed the Nomadic Pastoralists from simple pillagers or exploiters of the wealth accumulated by sedentary Rural Craftsman societies into invincible warriors and reformers burning with sacred fury. Under such circumstances, the victim ceased to be viewed primarily as the object of plunder, and was looked upon instead as an infidel whose very existence was offensive to God. Pastoral peoples invigorated by this new civilizational process fell upon their neighbors with unparalleled enthusiasm, and trained themselves and their horses for the most daring exploits, fortified by faith in their mission to eradicate impiety and heresy from the world.

Despotic Salvationist Empires

Although handicapped by failure to formulate a universal cult, the first of these salvationist expansions was able to dynamize a group of Iranian peoples, the Sassanian Persians, transforming them into the founders of a vast empire—that for centuries dominated Iran and Mesopotamia, and extended as far as India—and into propagators of the Mazdian religion, which exerted its influence as far east as China. Although the doctrine of Mazdianism, based on the teachings of Zarathustra (Zoroaster of the Greeks), had been compiled in a sacred book known as the Avesta during the Achaemenian domination, it only achieved the stature of a state religion and a messianic movement under the Sassanians. Beginning in the first quarter of the third century A.D., the latter expanded over Asia Minor with extraordinary vigor, destroying the Hellenistic influence that had become dominant in the region, restoring ancient Iranian traditions, and imposing the Mazdian faith. The Sassanian Empire was structured as a religious state, with a bureaucracy that exacted fiscal support from the subjugated populations along with combating heresies. The agricultural system was based on provisional concession of lands and peasant villages to a military nobility, an arrangement that assured their subordination to the central power.

A more mature expression of salvational expansionism was achieved during the 7th century, when Islam mobilized the energies of the pastoral peoples of Arabia and Iran to launch the greatest religious crusade known to history. Its basic inspiration came from the ancient pastoral tradition of plunder of lands and goods, now fortified by a sense of holy destiny. The Mohammedan doctrine, gathered together in the Koran, synthesized earlier

Jewish, Hellenic, and Iranian traditions, and amalgamated them into a new universal religion that was oriented more strongly than any previous one toward proselytization by conquest in the interest of divine glorification. As a messianic creed, Islam placed greater emphasis on physical expansion of the domain of Allah over all the peoples of the world than it did on efforts to save souls from perdition. The view of paradise as a haven of rest for the holy warrior reflects this orientation. The political and religious systems were fused by attributing to each able-bodied man a multiple destiny: as a crusading suppressor of infidel peoples, as a colonizer of conquered areas, and as a holy arm for enforcing submission to Allah. As a consequence, there did not develop a state-church organization with a professional body of priests.

This spirit of sacred mission filled Moslem Arab warriors with divine zeal and impelled them in all directions with the force of an avalanche, which innumerable feudalized societies were helpless to resist. It also infused the Moslems with a capacity to withstand acculturation when they came into contact with more highly evolved cultures. Above all, it instilled in them the strength necessary to consolidate conquered peoples into immense despotic imperial systems, which were integrated by a new moral order sanctioned by the word of the Prophet. In a few decades, Moslem domination overran most of the Middle East; from there it expanded westward over northern Africa, the Mediterranean islands, and the Iberian peninsula, and eastward over the Asian steppe to India, Indochina, and Indonesia. Later, it penetrated deeply into tropical Africa on the one hand, and into Eurasia and the frontiers of China on the other. These last waves were propelled by proselytized populations like the Turkish Mongols, who became the most dynamic force of Islamic expansion.

Islam was disseminated in this manner over a much more extensive area than that embraced by any previous imperial civilization, and with much more lasting effects because of the unprecedented power of assimilation and compulsory acculturation it was able to exert over conquered peoples. Its domination over Iberia, exercised through the Califate of Córdoba, lasted from A.D. 750 to 1350; that over India endured six centuries, first under the Sultanate of Delhi (1300–1526) and then under the Timurid Empire (1530–1705). Even after these states fell into feudal regression, the peoples over which they had exercised domination in the

Near East, northern Africa, tropical Africa, and Eurasia remained transfigured. The result was one of the most extensive modern cultural historical configurations, incorporating more than 300 million souls.

During the course of this prodigious expansion, the Islamized peoples, many of whom had been pastoralists with simple cultures, advanced to a high level of civilization. Interspersed between the great centers of antiquity, they were able to blend elements from several traditions into a new and more advanced culture, and later to act as the civilizers of both Orient and Occident. Creation of a vast network of imperial domination and religious subjugation permitted them to operate as agents of one of the most vigorous civilizational processes of all time, with a capacity for the incorporation of backward peoples and modernization of their technology, society, and ideological values otherwise achieved only in the course of the subsequent Mercantile and Industrial Revolutions.

The primary mechanisms of expansion and compulsory acculturation were conquest, subjugation of the most despotic type, enslavement, religious indoctrination, and racial mixture. Integration was initially accomplished by eliminating the dominant stratum of the conquered society and substituting a new bureaucratic layer that was initially composed of soldiers responsible for the control and exploitation of extensive areas. Later, their place was taken by groups of functionaries who had been carefully trained to carry out the duties of politico-military domination, administration of economic activities, and tax collection. Preparation of this bureaucracy drew upon the experience gained in nomadic pastoral life, including the application of practices developed for animal training to the exploitation of human slaves. Captive children selected for their physical stamina were placed in special establishments, where they underwent a meticulous training course designed both to stimulate a high degree of ambition and competitive spirit and to develop maximum levels of skill.

Although despotic, this method of preparation was based on the widest recruitment system that could be desired, and on an educational discipline unobtainable by any other process. In practice, it permitted the formation of castes of functionaries and soldiers of remarkable efficiency. Although membership involved dehumanization and alienation, it also offered an opportunity for individuals from subjugated populations to achieve careers of such brilliance that the competition to enter the training establishments far overran any opposition to the system. Super-specialized slaves were trained to exercise functions of the most disparate types, ranging from eunuch guardians for the harems, through artisans, political advisers, and scholars to high functionaries who could not only act as tax collectors for their sultan, but who could even reach the position of grand vizier. Above all, however, there were produced highly trained soldiers, who although they might attain the highest levels of power and wealth, always remained affiliated with the slave class and thus under the control of their masters.

The existence of these highly specialized agents of Islamic domination made it possible to maintain for centuries a power that could not have been sustained by simple soldiers inflamed with divine fury alone. After conquest and pillage, the trained agents organized the new territorial possessions and civilized the people, including the conquered soldiers. Because this organizational task, along with colonization and the introduction of new productive techniques, required other skills than zeal for combat, educational institutions were created and expanded until they became the normal method of preparing military and administrative teams.

Characteristics like these make it necessary to label this sociocultural formation as despotic and salvationistic. From classic to modern times, the former adjective has been improperly applied to formations based on irrigation, which are said to be characterized by "Oriental despotism." Although elements of despotism appear in these and other formations, it is only in the Despotic Salvationist Empires that they reach a sufficient degree of expression to justify their selection as a diagnostic trait.

The influence of the Despotic Salvationist Empires was extended beyond the limits of their direct domination by diffusion of both the technology and the patterns of sociopolitical organization. It also manifested itself indirectly in the defensive measures taken by peoples threatened with attack. Examples are the unsuccessful attempt to break down European feudalism by creation of the Germanic Holy Roman Empire and the eruption of the Crusades. The militarization of Byzantine society and its subsequent crystallization into an empire was another reaction to Islamic hostility, initially of Arabian-Iranian and later of Turco-Mongoloid origin. Europe experienced a similar dynamization for a brief period with the appearance of the Carlovingian Empire. All these developments took the form of incipient Despotic Salvationist Empires.

New salvationist movements occurred between the 10th and 13th centuries in the form of the Crusades, which represented the first wave of western European expansion. They were inspired, however, less by salvationistic fervor than by ambitions for conquest and wealth on the part of French feudal lords and of burghers in the developing Italian cities. Thousands of European peasants deserted their homes and set forth with their wives and children for the Holy Land, constituting a disorganized, unarmed, and ragged army that supported itself by begging and pillage. It was only later that the Crusades became a more disciplined and effective military undertaking, with the goal of conquering Islamic domains that by then had fallen into a feudal condition. Aroused by these attacks, the Moslems swiftly liquidated the military colonies established by the crusaders throughout the Near East, thereby terminating the first cycle of European Christian salvationist expansionism.

The Byzantine Empire (1025–1453), also modeled on a Despotic Salvationist pattern, was a response to Islamic opposition toward expansion of Orthodox Christianity in the Orient. It was able to attain a higher level of integration than comparable European efforts (e.g., Carlovingian Empire) because the requirements for defense against the Arabs, Iranians, and Turks strengthened the militaristic imperial state to the extent that it could counteract sedition by local feudal lords and oppose the trend toward feudalism. The price of this opposition was the structuring of Byzantine society as a Despotic Salvationist formation, initially Christian and subsequently Islamic, after the Turks installed themselves in Constantinople. After that time, its despotic salvationist characteristics came to full maturity.

In all the areas dominated by Despotic Salvationist Empires, the same basic social order was established. Among its principal features were (1) cession of land to the victors for their lifetime use, first without the right of transmission, but later as freely alienable property; (2) concession to the same groups of the functions of collecting imperial taxes on land and persons; (3) adoption of slavery of the Greco-Roman type and serfdom of the Russian type for mining and commercial agricultural activities; (4) encouragement of free foreign trade, but with the products subject to state control and confiscation; (5) development of large state factories where craftsmen produced luxury articles and weapons; (6) establishment of official monopolies based on imperial concessions for the exploitation of certain types of production; and (7) the creation of a vast system of census records on the populations of dominated areas and the levy of tribute, frequently by means of auction or lease of the rights to collect taxes and duties.

As they achieved stability, these empires were led, like earlier ones, first to decomposition through disputes between sultanates and chiefdoms of different ethnic origins, and later to feudalization. Resurgence into local power by rural proprietors and the concessioners of monopolies and tribute collection further diluted the central authority. As these dissociative forces became more accentuated, salvationist fervor was correspondingly weakened, to be replaced by a growing religious tolerance. The reason was basically economic: since newly converted Moslems were exempt from the payment of certain kinds of tribute, religious conversion brought a decline in state revenues. In spite of such disruptive factors, the absence of an external military force able to challenge their highly trained armies allowed the isolated sultanates to survive for centuries and to maintain strong compulsive powers over their domains.

World

Civilizations

The Mercantile Revolution

At the dawn of the 16th century, the progressive development of productive and military technology culminated in the Mercantile Revolution, which in turn brought about the maturation of two new sociocultural formations: the Salvationistic Mercantile Empires and the Capitalistic Mercantile Empires. This new technological revolution stemmed principally from advances in oceanic navigation achieved by combining improved instruments of orientation (magnetic compass, quadrant, astrolabe, celestial charts, maps, chronometers, etc.) with better means of navigation (warships and caravels, lateen sail, fixed rudder, etc.). Other contributing factors were mechanical inventions such as the crank piston rod and the Cardan shaft, and revolutionary advances in metallurgy resulting from the discovery of industrial processes for iron smelting, steel rolling, wire making, and alloying, as well as the development of screw vises and machines for shaping, grinding, and polishing metal. Concomitantly, the arts of war were renovated by the introduction of improved firearms (cannons, mortars, shotguns), which made it possible to challenge the mobility of cavalries armed only with bows and lances, and to create a naval artillery at sea. Expansion into general use of such inventions as improved types of windmills with movable tops and gravity-propelled, horizontal hydraulic wheels to drive bellows, hammers, saws, grinders, and other machines, was another significant factor, along with the appearance of paper-making factories, printing presses with movable type, and optical instruments. The combination of some of these innovations, such as sailing ships with cannons, led to extraordinary consequences; by permitting domination of the land from the sea, they introduced a new type of marine power. This new technology, developed almost exclusively in regions dominated by the Despotic Salvationist Empires, permitted the first real rupture of feudalism, originating as it did from forces generated within feudalized areas rather than from external attack by pastoral peoples.

The potential of the new technological revolution was realized through two successive but interrelated civilizational processes. The first led to the creation and expansion of the Salvationistic Mercantile Empires by a reconquest of the territory once dominated by Despotic Salvationist Empires. The second brought a maturation of secular restorative efforts in feudalized Europe with the establishment of the Capitalistic Mercantile Empires. Both kinds of empire contrasted with previous formations in their world-wide character, which expressed itself both in geographical expansion over the whole world and in a capacity to thwart the parallel development of other civilizational processes.

Salvationistic Mercantile Empires and Slavistic Colonies

Salvationistic Mercantile Empires arose during the 15th and 16th centuries in Spain and Russia, both of which were geographically and culturally marginal to Europe. In both regions, the energies that had been mobilized to drive the Arabs and Mongol-Tartars from their territories were rechanneled into salvationistic expansions. The Iberian peninsula, projecting physically into the Atlantic, was the jumping-off point for conquest and subjugation of new worlds beyond the sea. Portugal, which had been exploring the African coast since the beginning of the 15th century, discovered Cape Verde and the Gold Coast, rounded the Cape of Good Hope, and finally opened a sea route to India. There it first subjugated the western coast and then part of the eastern coast of India and Malacca. It also occupied Aden and Ormuz, obstructing the ancient spice route, and took possession of the Sunda archipelago, Indochina, and Brazil. Meanwhile, Spain reached the Antilles with the expeditions of Columbus, and expanded from there over much of the American continent; it also planted colonies and trading posts in the Far East. Russia, on the eastern extremity of Europe, expanded over the Eurasian continent and reached into America with the occupation of Alaska. This European explosion, which produced the first world civilization, was not an independent phenomenon, however, but the offspring of technological innovations and social institutions of Islamic origin.

Both Iberia and Russia had undergone centuries of foreign occupation. Iberia, the western bastion of Moorish domination, had struggled for freedom since the 13th century, but achieved success only in the year that

America was discovered. This war of emancipation required such extreme sacrifice that the whole society was transformed by its pursuit. Religious orders became richer and more powerful than the nobility, special corps of soldier-priests were created, and the Catholic Church took possession of a large part of the land recovered from the infidels. The association between the Iberian monarchs and the Papacy was so close as almost to constitute a fusion of the economic resources and salvationism of Madrid with the anti-reform zeal of Rome. Under this state of affairs, Iberia obtained from the Pope the title to exclusive domination over all lands discovered west of an imaginary line, and the Spanish monarchy was granted the privileges of creating and directing the Sacred Inquisition, of conferring the title of "apostolic vicar" with the status of "universal patronage," and even of collecting tithes and other Church income. In this way, an aristocratic-ecclesiastical power structure was established that henceforth controlled the destinies of the Iberian people.

Victory over Islam also destroyed the agrarian system introduced by the Moors. This system was based on a highly developed irrigation agriculture, which for centuries had permitted the maintenance of a dense population in even the most arid zones. Under the new aristocratic-ecclesiastical rulers, regions once intensively cultivated were converted into pasture for sheep, replacing abundance with poverty. Concomitantly, large numbers of peasants were expelled from the land and reduced to begging, and the population as a whole drastically declined both in the country and in the city. Not even all the gold taken from America during succeeding centuries could prevent this recession, because its basic cause lay in the configuration developed by the Salvationistic Mercantile Empire on the Iberian peninsula. Although capable of absorbing and generalizing the technology of the Mercantile Revolution and consequently of becoming one of the sources of capitalism, Iberia retained archaic and anachronistic features that precluded its successful competition with mature capitalistic formations.

Muscovite Russia developed its ethnic-national profile out of the Rural Craftsman State stage under the stimulus of Mongol-Tartar domination, and its ruling class grew in size and wealth by serving as tribute collector for the Golden Horde. When it finally achieved emancipation after decades of fighting (that here too required total mobilization of national resources), it also took an anachronistic form that was incapable of fully capitalistic development.

The cultural configurations of these two Salvationistic Mercantile Empires were thus deeply impregnated not only with elements retained from the Despotic Salvationist traditions that had dominated their peoples for centuries, but also with characteristics developed during the course of opposition to that domination. On the ideological level, this led to messianic movements for the expansion of Christianity that resembled spontaneous crusades. With a religious fanaticism comparable only to that inspiring the first Islamic impetus, Iberia assigned to its *conquistadores* the dual role of despoiler and crusader. It undertook with equal fervor the eradication of heresies among its own population (by ordering the flogging of those suspected of impiety, public festivals for the burning of heretics, etc.) and the expulsion of hundreds of thousands of Moors and Jews who had lived on the peninsula for centuries under Saracen rule. This exodus provided the dominant class with an extraordinary opportunity to acquire wealth by the confiscation of Moslem and Jewish property. It also led to a severe economic recession because not only were the heretics expelled from Iberia, but along with them a considerable number of artisans, small farmers, and traders who made up a large portion of the "infidel castes." Elimination of this social stratum led to an immediate deterioration in the technical level of agriculture and manufacturing activities, and also broke down the national system of commercial exchange, creating a situation that contributed decisively to the inability of Spain and Portugal to participate in the Industrial Revolution.

Russian expansion took on more of a despotic than a salvationistic character. It also, however, was motivated by Christian fervor, which expressed itself in the effort to create a "Third Rome," in the integration of the Patriarch of Moscow into Czarism, in secular efforts to Christianize the population, in the mystic character of Russian religion, in a tremendous expansion of the clergy (comparable only to what occurred in Iberia), and in religious intolerance, which later manifested itself more severely in the *pogroms*.

In the socio-economic organization of the two empires, mercantile principles of oriental-despotic inspiration prevailed over those of incipient capitalism. As a result, a vast bureaucracy for control of politico-military power and for collection of tribute was erected in both areas over and above the bourgeois-capitalistic empresariat. State monopolies expanded over various productive sectors, and private businesses were increasingly subjected to governmental interference. In both regions, mines and factories; salt, diamond, and tobacco enterprises; external commerce, and many other sectors were controlled by the state, which also collected tribute and dispensed rewards and titles. The resources obtained from all these activities supported huge bodies of priests, financed the construction of innumerable temples, and defrayed the expenses of the military and administrative machinery—which operated as a vast patronage system.

The Ibero-American colonial empires were structured as a counterpart to this Salvationistic Mercantile formation by the process of historical incorporation, which shaped them into a new kind of slavistic colonialism. They were inserted into a unified and interacting system, not as representatives of an earlier evolutionary stage, but as complementary parts of a complex in which the Iberian powers formed the dynamic center and the colonial populations the peripheral areas and "external proletariats." The striking similarities between Iberian slavistic colonialism and the earlier Greco-Roman or Carthaginian form are thus to be explained by their common derivation via processes of historical incorporation generated by different civilizations, rather than by viewing them as necessary steps in cultural evolution.

The basic procedures of domination employed by the Slavistic Colonies in the Americas were (1) eradication of the former local ruling class; (2) concession of land to the conquerors under the *latifundia* system; (3) adoption of slavistic forms of labor conscription; and (4) implantation of patriarchal bureaucracies to represent the royal power and with the authority to collect taxes.

In Mesoamerica and the central Andes, where Theocratic Irrigation Empires had existed and where labor was both available in large concentrations and disciplined for work, slavery became institutionialized in the *mita* and *encomienda*. Under this form of conscription, the Indians were subjected to the most inhumane kind of exploitation, which was justified on the grounds that eternal salvation was being brought to them through the catechismal function of the *encomenderos*. Later, the *encomienda* allowed tribute to be paid in money, which the Indians could only obtain by working in the mines and fields under the most arduous conditions. In order that this increasingly oppressive slavistic regime could operate, native chiefs were assigned the task of securing able-bodied labor for exploitation by the *encomenderos*, their cooperation being rewarded by allowing elderly people and children to remain living in the villages.

Under the influence of European diseases and broken by the weight of toil, the indigenous population declined so alarmingly that depopulation of the colonies became a serious preoccupation of the Crown. There was fear of the economic disaster that could result from loss of the seemingly inexhaustible supply of cheap labor and its replacement by a new caste, the mestizos, who were resistant to enslavement and prone to rebellious tendencies, and who furthermore lacked a traditional place in the racially stratified society. In addition to being reduced numerically, the indigenous population was progressively degraded by having to serve not only as a mere labor force, but as one that did not exist for its own benefit but only for the production of the few kinds of articles that were of interest to the colonial economy and, especially, for the extraction of precious metals. As a result of this submergence into a spurious culture, the high level of technology that had been attained aboriginally disappeared. In other parts of the Americas, the Greco-Roman form of slavery was restored in its most brutal form, first with the enslavement of the indigenous population and later, when this was depleted, with the transplantation of large numbers of Negroes from Africa to work the plantations and mines.

This was the greatest movement of historical incorporation that has ever occurred, involving the detribalization and deculturation of millions of Indians and Negroes and their subsequent integration into new economic systems in the form of subordinate classes. Highly oppressive conditions of compulsive acculturation were created, which welded these neo-Americans into the Spanish and Portuguese macro-ethnos as a vast "external proletariat" of common laborers. That the deculturative power of this process of historical incorporation was greater than that of equivalent Romanization and Islamization processes is evident in the linguistic and cultural uniformity of the Latin American peoples, who are much more homogeneous than the population of the Iberian peninsula in spite of being both more numerous and more widely dispersed.

Throughout Ibero-America, the Church re-assumed the role and function that it had exercised in Medieval Europe and became the major holder of lands, Indians, and mortgages. Its wealth came directly from the Crown in the form of tithes, donations, bequests, and special rights, including Inquisitorial extortion. The latter could be applied to anyone suspected of heresy and permitted the confiscation of all goods, rights of inheritance, and balances due on loans (cf. Lea, 1908; Lewin, 1962).

The Russian expansion was much less vigorous, and was patterned more closely on the pre-existing despotic formation. As a result, conquered lands and estates were not distributed in the form of private property. Instead, privileges were granted to the nobility and clergy for the collection of tribute from the peasants. By the time these concessions were replaced by hereditary land ownership, the most severe kinds of servitude had given way to new forms of regulation that kept the peasantry under the control of private landlords. The greater poverty of the area under Russian exploitation, as well as the smaller size and greater cultural backwardness of the populations involved, made maintenance of this system imperative. There was no opportunity either for the appearance of a structure of small farmers in the conquered areas or for economic prosperity equal to that attained by the Iberian colonial enterprises.

Under these circumstances, instead of advancing technologically and institutionally to mature capitalistic forms of production and social organization, the two Salvationistic Mercantile Empires developed increasingly despotic tendencies in their colonial domains. At the same time, their metropolitan areas were prone to episodic dips into feudal regressions whenever imperial authority was supplanted by that of the landed nobility and the clergy.

Capitalistic Mercantile Empires and Modern Colonialism

While salvationistic expansion was still in progress, the renovating forces of the Mercantile Revolution were proceeding via another civilizational process to create a new sociocultural formation: the Capitalistic Mercantile Empires. Although initially poorer than the Salvationistic Mercantile formation, this held greater potentialities for social reorganization and technological advancement. So dynamic was its force, in fact, that regional economies that had stagnated in feudalism for a millennium were stimulated into activity, first on the European continent and later throughout the world. A series of events, coupled with the adoption of new technical and institutional procedures, permitted a resurgence of manufacturing in Italian, French, Belgian, and Dutch cities, and later in England and Spain—first for internal consumption and later for export. As markets expanded, the manufacturing establishments grew from small groups of artisans, who owned their own tools and were financed by a capitalist, into large concerns with an internal division of labor and a proprietor, who owned the equipment, paid salaries to the workmen, and enjoyed the profits of their toil.

Initially, these centralized establishments appeared in rural areas where they could escape control by urban artisan guilds. Peasants were employed first in spinning and weaving; later, in sawmills, sugar refineries, and soap, paint, and beer factories; and still later in shipbuilding, metalworking, and paper-making operations. Monetary wealth accumulated through commerce, usury, and the investment of public funds. State monopolies began to embrace manufacturing, gradually luring the factories to the cities, which began to grow again. The demand for produce and goods to feed and clothe the urbanized workers expanded the internal market for agricultural and manufactured products. Rural proprietors, interested in taking advantage of this growing market, began to coerce the peasants into greater productivity and to expel from their lands the old patriarchal clientele that consumed the major part of the harvest. In several areas, this process culminated in the conversion of the cultivated lands into pasture for sheep raising and wool production.

At this point, the governments began to encourage these activities, which were becoming a major source of public income. Support was provided in the form of protective tariffs and of reforms in those institutions that restricted either the freedom to obtain labor or the expansion of the internal market. The ancient norms that had impeded commercialization of agricultural production were overthrown. Fencing of land was permitted, and this put an end to communal fields and to traditional pasture rights. Community structure, which had been dominated by subsistence activities and relations of mutuality, was broken down by the expansion of contractual labor relations. Driven by the necessity to provide themselves with food and clothing, increasingly larger rural contingents voluntarily or involuntarily abandoned the subsistence economy and entered into salaried work. Karl Marx (1965, pp. 110–111) described this process well when he wrote:

> . . . when the great English landowners dismissed their retainers, who had consumed a share of their surplus produce of their land; when their farmers drove out the small cottagers, etc., then a doubly free mass of living labour power was thrown on to the *labour market:* free from the old relation of clientship, villeinage or service, but also free from all goods and chattels, from every real and objective form of existence, *free from all property*. Such a mass would be reduced

either to the sale of its labour power or to beggary, vagabondage and crime, but was herded off this road on to the narrow path which led to the labour market by means of gallows, pillory and whip.

The peasant reaction to this structural reform was expressed in wars to defend the old *modus vivendi,* or in demands for ownership of the lands by those who worked them. In attacking the constituted order, their only model was an idealized past when goodness and justice prevailed. The irreducible conflict between their own interests and those of the principal landowning monopoly, the Church, often forced them into an anti-clerical position. In this atmosphere of social change, everything became a cause. The social order ceased to be viewed as sacred, or the sacredness of its character was re-appraised. As a result, mechanisms for preservation of the regime were weakened, favoring the spread of peasant insurrections as capitalism advanced from region to region.

Beginning in the 13th century, Europe was convulsed by successive waves of uprisings, such as that of the Pastors (1251) and Plebeus (1320) in the Low Countries and France; of Dolcino (1305) in Italy; of Marcel and La Jacquerie (1357) in France; and of Wat Tylor (1381) in England. In the 15th century, the Husites rebelled in Bohemia, and other peasant uprisings occurred in Germany. When the process reached more distant regions, peasant wars also exploded there, as for example in Russia in the 17th (Razin), 18th (Pugachov), and 19th centuries. Such movements were doomed to fail because they originated from the subordinate class, which could not reorganize the entire society in accord with its own interests. They played a decisive role, however, in the establishment of a new capitalistic-mercantile order, in the victory of religious reformation movements, and in the creation of a power structure headed by capitalistic entrepreneurs.

A simultaneous process of uprooting and relocation of workers took place in the cities, releasing the artisans from the corporate ties of the guilds and converting them into salaried employees of new businesses. In country after country, conversion of the economy to capitalism resulted in the abolition of trade societies, apprenticeships, and wage unions. All such protective institutions were replaced by "equality before the law and by free contractual rights."

The availability of labor, capital, and subsistence goods for sale made possible the establishment of urban structures for production and commerce, which grew to dominate the whole economic system, converting it into a Capitalistic Mercantile formation. This civilizational process was stimulated to prodigious acceleration by the fruits of Iberian oceanic expansion. The Capitalistic Mercantile Empires achieved rapid maturity, propelled first by the produce pillaged from dozens of conquered peoples, and later by the surplus extracted from the labor of millions of slaves. They failed to crystallize, however, in either of the two areas where the Mercantile Revolution first took place, and where Salvationistic Mercantile Empires had subsequently developed. While the latter interacted with the new formation, their anachronistic structure condemned them to a declining importance in the developing mercantile economy.

The Capitalistic Mercantile Empire formation first appeared in Holland (1609) after the war of emancipation from the Iberian salvationistic domination had been won. During the course of this war, the Dutch took possession of a number of Portuguese and Spanish colonies in Africa (Cape of Good Hope), the Americas (Antilles), and the Orient (Ceylon and Indonesia), and became the principal European power. They then established the first modern banking organization (1609), which assumed the responsibility for financing and insuring Dutch mercantile expansion and soon became the agency for the distribution of world production in the European market. As a consequence, the Dutch social structure assumed the form of a modern republic, oligarchical in nature, and governed by merchants and bankers.

England followed when the Cromwell Revolution (1652–1679) forced restructuring into a Capitalistic Mercantile formation, which in this case was clothed in the institutional attributes of a constitutional monarchy. Her modernization was facilitated by the immigration of some hundred thousand religious refugees, who substantially raised both the caliber of her labor force and the availability of capital. The primary source of wealth in this initial stage, however, was state supported piracy, which was supplanted later by contraband with the American colonies. This contraband consisted principally of monopolistic contracts with the Iberian nations for exploitation of the slave trade, and was engaged in by official companies whose primary stockholders were the Spanish and English royal houses. The application of capitalistic efficiency to the slave traffic led to a more rational organization of operations for the capture of slaves, for their assembly in reservations on the African coast, for their maritime transportation, and for their storage, distribution, and sale throughout the Americas. During the course of nearly three centuries, the pioneer Capitalistic Mercantile nations of Europe gained possession of more than a hundred million Africans, a third of whom must have reached their destination, where they were consumed primarily in the slave market (Tannenbaum, 1947; Arnault, 1958; Williams, 1944).

The economic integration of France into the Capitalistic Mercantile formation took place slowly after the beginning of the 17th century with the installation in Lyon, Rheims, and Paris of factories for production of luxury articles, and later of printing and metallurgical plants. The new formation finally manifested itself on the political level with the social revolution of 1784, which was led initially by anti-aristocrats and then by a military regime that imposed the Napoleonic ordinances. The first state system of public education was created and the former legal order was replaced with liberal capitalistic institutions, which were rapidly adopted throughout the world. With the French annexation of colonies in North America, Indochina, and Senegal, this capitalistic formation also penetrated areas of former Spanish domination.

In order to achieve their pioneer position, these nations had to reactivate their internal economic life by breaking down the feudal barriers that restricted production. Ecclesiastical goods and the estates of abbeys and monasteries were confiscated and integrated into the productive system. Capital was invested in factories, and these began to produce first for the national market and later for export. Large investment houses were created to make available funds in excess of the financial capacities of an individual capitalist, and incentives were provided for the development of a highly trained labor force. As a consequence of these changes, social stratification was altered: A class of proprietors able to control salaried or slave labor developed in opposition to the dispossessed workers, and two distinct proletariats were created, one of them metropolitan and the other colonial. The maintenance and reproduction of these divergent but mutually complementary strata and their intrinsic antagonism, became significant forces in social dynamics.

In their overseas expansion, all the Capitalistic Mercantile formations fell back on slavistic colonialism for the creation of new areas of tropical plantations. They modified the old model, however, by initiating programs of mercantile colonization involving the establishment of trading posts in distant countries to maintain commercial relations with the indigenous populations rather than to transform them. Later, Immigrant Colonies were created by the transplantation of Europeans across the seas. Their principal purpose was to syphon off some of the population that had been rendered surplus by integration of the agricultural economy into capitalistic patterns, and whose existence at home had begun to represent a permanent threat of insurrection. As a consequence, the small Immigrant Colonies, which had been the least prosperous type under the preceding formation, began to expand.

In North America, such Immigrant Colonies, which had initially been peripheral to the rich slavistic colonial enterprises of the Antilles, matured rapidly into mercantile capitalism. The diagnostic features of the formation became more accentuated here than in any other colonial area because of the unique character of this transatlantic extension of English society. As a result, there arose in North America a modern federal republic that was structured as a Capitalistic Mercantile formation with tendencies toward industrialization. With enormous uninhabited areas readily accessible, the United States was slow to undertake colonialistic expansion. Ultimately, however, it appropriated areas of former Iberian domination, such as Puerto Rico and the Philippines, as well as several Pacific islands.

As has been shown, the Capitalistic Mercantile formation also assumed two complementary forms from the beginning: (1) The metropolitan form was represented by nations structured by evolutionary acceleration as centers of power and overseas commerce and had two kinds of internal support: (a) a rural economy composed either of free farmers who produced for the market (especially in France and the United States) or of large capitalistic agricultural and pastoral enterprises operated with salaried labor (especially in Germany and England); and (b) an urban commercial manufacturing economy made up of importers and financial agencies. (2) The colonial complex was implanted by movements of historical incorporation, and created (a) the Trading Colonies in the form of Asiatic trading posts and African slave suppliers, (b) the American Slavistic Colonies for mineral exploitation and commercial agriculture, which were administered directly or indirectly by other colonial agents such as the Portuguese or the Spanish, and (c) the Immigrant Colonies of the Americas, Australia, and New Zealand.

In both of these complementary forms, one metropolitan and the other colonial, operation of the system led to class differentiation. In the metropolitan form, capitalists were distinguished from the growing body of wage-earners; in the colonial form, managers were differentiated from the enslaved or subjugated masses. In terms of the system, the latter were not really workers, but merely a source of energy equivalent to later inanimate sources (Marx, 1965, p. 41). This dehumanized condition permitted a much larger accumulation of capital than could be obtained through the exploitation of wage labor, and it provided ever greater investment returns to the metropolitan economies possessing mature capitalistic structures.

European overseas expansion, which had been pioneered by the Iberian nations, now became a general activity. Multiplication of Trading, Slavistic, and Immigrant Colonies throughout the world accelerated the Capitalistic and Mercantile civilizational processes, leading to the most extensive movement of historical incorporation that has ever occurred. Millions of people were transplanted from one continent to another, the most divergent races were intermingled, and the most disparate cultural traditions were affected and remodeled. This cultural interchange, which was most pronounced on the technological level, provided the first basis for the re-unification of human culture. It did so by incorporating into a world economy as subordinate societies with spurious cultures thousands of peoples bound to tribal, village, pastoral, or rural craftsman formations, or to ancient civilizations (those still vigorous as well as those stagnating in feudal regressions). In this new context, perpetuation of their own way of life ceased to be the motivation for existence; such peoples become instead coefficients of existence and instruments of prosperity for the metropolitan centers that had assumed control of their destinies. Their despoiling permitted the European cities not only to regain but greatly to surpass the brilliance that had been attained at the height of the Roman Empire. This acquisition of power imbued the Nordic Europeans, who until this time had been marginal to the civilizational process, with a sense of superiority and civilizing mission that served as a justification for any kind of colonial oppression.

The wealth accumulated from new productive activities and the plunder of foreign treasure stimulated development of the monetary economy to new heights, and made increasing amounts of capital available to finance new enterprises. In the period between 1591 and 1660, Spain took from America 4537.6 tons of gold, while Portugal extracted from Brazil alone during the 18th century some 1400 tons of gold and 3 million carats of diamonds. The Mexican contribution raised world silver production from

335 tons between 1701 and 1720 to 879 tons between 1781 and 1800. This marked increase in the availability of precious metals led to continuously rising prices, resulting in disorganization of the surviving peasant economies. As a consequence, new groups were thrown onto the labor market or obliged to emigrate, and a capitalistic outlook replaced the former conservatism.

Simultaneously, Europe was ideologically transfigured through the maturation of a secular movement initiated with the Renaissance and intensified with the Reformation. In those areas where mercantile capitalism was most advanced, the old religious hierarchies were overthrown. Literacy was extended from Latin to the spoken languages to permit reading of the Bible by the common man. The effect was to make intellectual pursuits accessible to a larger portion of the populace and so to assure greater freedom of inquiry and investigation. As a result, post-Medieval Europe rediscovered Greek achievements in learning and the arts, as well as the earlier Mercantile Slavistic forms of political structure with their democratic content, which were restored and carried forward.

In areas where the Capitalistic Mercantile system had reached its greatest maturity, the Catholic Church lost its autonomous power and administrative authority. Reduced to an auxiliary institution, the Church became responsible only for shaping the conscience of the individual. It was soon called upon, however, to provide spiritual reinforcement for the new class structure. Reform theologians devoted themselves to the formulation of an ideology that enobled wealth (considered to be a sign of divine favor), dignified work, and condemned idleness among the upper class and begging, its lower class counterpart. The spiritual authority of the Reform Church helped the incipient middle class to adopt the new ethic and to destroy the moral basis of the former system—in which property was conceived as incorporating duties rather than rights, and in which the rigid social stratification of feudal Europe was accepted as an expression of divine will (Weber, 1948).

With mercantile capitalism, the foundations were thus laid for impersonalization of labor relations, for treating labor as a negotiable commodity, for exalting a new type of managerial class with prescribed rights rather than obligations, and for establishing an economic regime of an exceedingly opportunistic and venal nature. Freed of religious impediments, the sciences and arts underwent an unparalleled development, laying the foundations for a new technological revolution. Medieval ordinances were renovated by a generation of free thinkers, who applied the most generous concepts of liberty and equality to the rational regulation of human relations, with full confidence in the continuation of human progress. Concomitantly, the first step was taken in the transition from an administration of people, which prevailed in the feudal world, to an administration of things, which characterizes capitalism. This alteration was achieved, however, only by objectifying people so that they could be legally treated as objects.

In its fully mature form, the new sociocultural formation was based on private enterprise involving the most bitter form of competition, a regime of economic spontaneity, and a total irresponsibility for the social welfare of the workers. It reinstated in accentuated form the despoiling and alienating tendencies that had emerged with the inception of social stratification, and which had been elaborated to extremes, first in the Mercantile Slavistic formation, and later in the Despotic Salvationist and Salvationistic Mercantile formations. As these disruptive concomitants of the Mercantile and Capitalistic civilizational processes began to grow in intensity, the European populations became subjects instead of agents of the forces of renovation. Social wealth grew to levels previously unattainable, but the poverty of the dispossessed classes also reached unparalleled extremes. European populations increased more rapidly than the demands of the system for additional labor, creating large human "surpluses" that had to be exported in the form of emigrants.

The Immigrant Colonies resulting from this process were expanded by several types of involuntary migration. Indentured servants of English, Irish, German, and other national extractions were exported to America and sold at auction to masters whom they served for four to six years without any other recompense than their food, clothing, and shelter. Supplementing these indentured servants were criminals condemned by English justice for delinquency or vagrancy, and individuals enticed by a variety of other methods. Those facing the worst conditions were the redemptioners, who had no fixed time limit on their period of service, or occasionally no limit at all, and thus were virtual slaves. Such enslaved European contingents represented between sixty-six and eighty percent of the labor force in the northern colonies. As new countries were incorporated into the Capitalistic Mercantile sphere, the same methods of recruitment were subsequently applied to other European groups. The system spread ultimately to Asia, where it resulted in a removal to the plantations of Australia, Africa, and America of Chinese and Indian "coolies" in the form of indentured servants (Bagú, 1949; Williams, 1944).

Although the Mercantile Revolution generated the greatest expansionist movement of human history and tended to unite the entire world into a single system of economic exchange, it also led to segmentation into hostile ethnic-national entities. Paradoxically, the civilizational process that had expanded over the whole world and had broken down internal regional barriers, came to a stop at national frontiers. Throughout Europe the ethnic-national nuclei that had begun to evolve following the dissolution of the Roman Empire began to take shape as modern nations. Each one corresponded to a community that for generations had shared the same beliefs and customs, but whose members now began to feel a solidarity that excluded outsiders and to assert political domination over the territory they occupied or felt to be theirs.

After centuries of slow development characterized by many population fusions, these ethnos finally attained an awareness of their identity by virtue of efforts on the part of the political system to reserve its monopoly over the national market. Under the influence of economic and political forces, the intelligentsia began to enhance the national self-image through the production of literary works in the vernacular. These emphasized the value of national traditions, the qualities of national heroes, and the superiority of blood ties. By such processes of organization and nationalistic affirmation, ethnic-national entities assumed the economic and social configurations within which their populations would henceforth live out their destinies. Those that achieved the earliest state structure and attained the highest development of capitalist economy began to expand, assimilating immature local and regional groups, and conquering and subjugating more advanced ones. Three centuries of crises, tensions, revolutions, and wars were required to shape the European ethnic panorama; during this time the rest of the world was transformed into an outlet for pillage and exploitation (cf. Znaniecki, 1944; Gennep, 1922; Kohn, 1945).

THE INDUSTRIAL REVOLUTION

The civilizational processes set in motion by the Mercantile Revolution were still actively operating when the Industrial Revolution began, and in turn initiated two new civilizational processes that crystallized distinct sociocultural formations. In its capacity to reorganize human societies, this new revolution can only be compared with the Agricultural Revolution some 10,000 years earlier. Like the latter, it was to affect every society, increasing the power of those that achieved industrialization to previously unimaginable heights, and subjecting those that did not to ever more insidious and imperious forms of domination. It was to remodel internally every society, whether industrialized directly or modernized indirectly; to alter social stratification and along with it the power structure; and profoundly to change the world view and system of values. The most critical effect of the new technological revolution, however, was to lay the foundation for a future, unified civilization by making the same basic technology accessible to all peoples, by incorporating them into the same forms of social organization, and by integrating them into a single system of values. Although this universal civilization would not be attained in the course of the Industrial Revolution, it became the general aspiration of people everywhere during this time.

Like previous civilizational processes, the effects of the Industrial Revolution were not spread by free and voluntary adoption, but rather through the reordering of peoples. Thus the pioneer industrialized nations assumed a superior position of wealth and domination, and the rest of the world became a vast subordinate complex of dependent and exploited nations. This new civilizational process had the special characteristic that, from its earliest and still markedly mercantile stages, it demonstrated an extraordinary power for historical incorporation. This permitted it to spread throughout the world and to envelope every nation and every individual with its compulsory forms of integration. Primitive peoples who had escaped the effects of the Mercantile Revolution were reached wherever they lived, and incorporated into the new economic and social order as the providers of agricultural and mineral raw materials and the consumers of industrial products.

The Industrial Revolution emerged out of the Capitalistic Mercantile formations by the accumulation of mechanical inventions that permitted a fantastic multiplication in the productivity of human labor. These formations had also undergone the most complete structural change during the Mercantile Revolution, bringing about the destruction of oligarchical resistance to changes in the *status quo*. Such mature conditions existed in England and in the United States, while France, Germany, and the Scandinavian countries were slightly less advanced. In the rest of Europe, the oligarchical structure, which was characterized by monopoly in land hold-ing, despotic social structure, and salvationistic survivals, remained pre-dominant.

The ruling class in sociocultural formations generated by the Industrial Revolution was the urban bourgeoisie, which had begun to increase in strength during the preceding stage and to force the reorganization of so-ciety in accord with its interests. Initially, this managerial class operated like the ancient merchants; i.e., through exploitation by usury, commercial speculation with scarce goods, monopolization of certain commodities, and maritime commerce. The Industrial Revolution created opportunities for new enterprises, however, which not only provided much greater profits in shorter periods of time, but also involved fewer risks than had sur-rounded speculative investment during the mercantile phase. Capital now became applied principally to exploitation of the new source of wealth represented by the factory system of mass production. Since this system was operated with inanimate sources of energy, its expansion required a radical modification of the social structure. Thus, the new technology made it not only possible but desirable to convert the work force, including slaves, into salaried labor. It also made it necessary to eliminate craft production, which still existed throughout the world, and to assign new functions to the displaced workers. At the same time, it became urgent to raise the levels of consumption so as to increase the market for industrial products essen-tial for continuous expansion of the factory system. As a consequence, the first impulses from the new technological revolution made obsolete the al-ready weakened Salvationistic Mercantile formations and destroyed the foundations of Capitalistic Mercantile ones by progressively absorbing their colonial content and wiping out slavery.

From the beginning of the 18th century, England had been expanding her naval power and the world-wide Capitalistic Mercantile system based thereon, and also accumulating technological applications of scientific principles to methods of production, both in factories and mines. When the industrial economy established in urban centers was applied to agricultural production, radical changes took place in the whole social structure, laying the foundation for the Industrial Revolution.

Technological renovation also led to the emergence of a new empre-sariat, which in turn promoted massive recruitment of unemployed artisans and displaced rural workers to operate the machinery in the factories. This development occurred in three stages. The first stage was marked by the invention and diffusion of steam engines, which used coal as fuel. Their application to the operation of mine pumps and elevators brought about a tremendous increase in coal production, while numerous industrial applications expanded the output of textile and metallurgical mills. The locomotive revolutionized land transportation, and the steamboat did the same on water. After 1820, increasingly efficient machines were developed in England, the United States, and France: their exportation to other parts of the world broadened the base over which industrial civilization could expand. The second stage began at the turn of the last century, when coal and steam were replaced by a more efficient method of energy conversion, namely, electricity obtained from water power. The third stage was attained with the development and diffusion of gasoline engines, which occurred principally after World War I.

During the course of this process, industrial production grew by leaps and bounds. Between 1860 and 1950, world coal production jumped from 132 to 1454 million tons; petroleum production rose from zero to 523 million tons; natural gas production from zero to 197 million cubic meters; and hydraulic power production from 6 to 332 million megawatt hours. Conversion of all these increases into megawatt hours yields the fantastic progression from 1079 to 20,556 million in only 90 years. Between 1870 and 1930, there was also marked acceleration in steel production, which rose from 30 to 180 million tons (Cipolla, 1962; Pasdermadjian, 1960; Ashton, 1948).

These innovations in industrial technology were supplemented by improvements in agriculture and animal breeding, both of which played a major role in the expansion of the food supply and thereby permitted the population to increase in newly modernized areas. Among the most important improvements in agriculture were generalization of techniques of annual cultivation to all arable land by rotation of crops and the use of fertilizers, refinements in methods of plowing, mechanization, seed selection, and pest extermination; simultaneously the genetic improvement of herds increased beef, milk, and wool production. These advances were accompanied by a world-wide diffusion of plants domesticated in the Americas, including a new type of cotton, but especially potatoes, maize, manioc, peanuts, cacao, tomatoes, and many other foods that greatly enriched the human diet.

For the first time in history, this new technological base created self-propelling systems of economic development, which henceforth accelerated the rates both of the productivity of human labor and of transformation in the social order. Urbanization was hastened, growing amounts of consumer goods became available in industrialized societies, and military power was continually increased. The result was emergence of the first "developed" countries with capitalistic industrial economies, whose supreme objective and prerequisite for existence became the constant expansion of their wealth and power through an increase in the productivity of labor, maximization of profits, and domination of the world market. The fundamental characteristic of this system became, henceforth, its compulsion for continuing technical progress and the accumulation of capital. Internally, these constituted the basis for survival of businesses, threatened on one side by competitors and on the other by the demands of their employees; externally, they were essential for maintenance of national autonomy in the competitive world market.

Imperialistic Industrial Powers and Neo-Colonial Dependencies

As its potentialities were realized, the first civilizational process to issue from the Industrial Revolution produced such profound changes in the ways of life of human societies that they became integrated into a single interacting system. This corresponded to a new sociocultural formation, which was bifurcated into two technologically unequal and economically opposed but nevertheless complementary complexes. The dominant one took shape by evolutionary acceleration, which transformed some Capitalistic Mercantile nations into centers of Imperialistic Industrial domination. The subordinate one resulted from movements of historical incorporation, which not only brought about redistribution of colonial areas among the new powers, but created a new form of dependence: Neo-Colonialism.

In the course of this civilizational process, the most despotic forms of colonial subjugation, such as slavery, were eliminated, but other forms of economic subordination were not only maintained but strengthened. The spoilative nature of the symbiotic relations between the center and the periphery now derived principally from the advantages that accrued to the highly developed systems during commercial exchanges with backward areas. The high level of mechanization and the use of inanimate energy in these industrial economies assured them of every advantage in trade relations with areas where the productive system still depended primarily on human labor. Furthermore, their enormous power of compulsion obliged those societies that had fallen into colonial and neo-colonial dependence to suffer all kinds of reflex transformations, which served to model them into more efficient servants for their despoilers. The world system thus became a symbiotic constellation, in which each component had its prescribed role, and in which expansion of either sector was accomplished within the framework of reciprocity between the colonialist nuclei and their areas of exploitation.

The first steps of the industrialization process were predominantly discordant and disruptive. Internally, the deleterious effects of the earlier capitalistic reorganization were aggravated: social differentiation increased, all remnants of the agrarian and artisan occupational classes were destroyed, and population growth expanded the contingents of unemployed. The rural exodus was intensified, causing enormous accumulation of marginal people in the cities. When these disruptive forces became sufficiently strong to threaten overthrow of the system, the governments applied increased pressure for emigration. This method of removal, coupled with population consumption via a series of wars, eliminated some 100 million people from Europe during the last century and a half, providing the safety valve essential to maintenance of the capitalistic industrial system. In spite of such measures, however, the European countries registered marked increases. In the period between 1800 and 1950, the English population grew from 16.2 to 50.6 million and the Italian one from 18.3 to 46.3 million (Sauvy, 1952–1954, 1961; Landry, 1949). If birth control had not come into general use at this time in industrialized nations, the increase would have been even larger.

England and France were the first nations to develop mature Imperialistic Industrial sociocultural formations. They were followed a little later by the United States, which had vast resources in virgin land and thus was able to absorb not only its own increasing population but large numbers of European immigrants into the labor force. Thanks to the constantly growing productivity of their labor and to erosion of their population surplus, the precociously industrialized nations were able to raise substantially their standard of living, to organize democratic parliamentary regimes that offered an opportunity for growing popular participation in political power, to provide public education for the entire population at the elementary level and, subsequently, to advance increasing numbers to intermediate and higher levels of education. Simultaneously, health was improved, life expectancy was increased, and new ideas of liberty, justice, and equality were formulated.

Externally, however, the process of industrialization operated as a movement of historical incorporation. As a result it promoted only a reflexive kind of modernization and imposed conditions of extreme hardship both on peoples already under colonial rule, and on those whose status had changed from the domains of the Salvationistic Mercantile Empires to the Neo-Colonial Dependencies of the great powers. These populations were drafted into the new productive system, the upper class in the capacity of a managerial body serving outside interests, and the masses as an "external proletariat" engaged in the production of raw materials. The last strongholds of slavery gave way to the new patterns of conscription of the labor force. This alteration could take place without an intervening decline into feudal regression because mercantile activities were intensified rather than interrupted, and also because the transition occurred during an intensive process of reflexive modernization. Only for short periods and in restricted areas, therefore, did some of the ex-slave populations revert to subsistence economies. In general, they were rapidly absorbed by the new modes of labor organization, all of which were highly exploitive and incipiently capitalistic.

Under the domination of industrial imperialism, the role of backward peoples was no longer to provide treasure for pillage, or to supply the world market with gold, silver, and spices or classic tropical products like sugar. Now their function was to furnish industrial raw materials such as minerals, oil, rubber, cotton, hides, wool, and various other products, which were produced principally by salaried workers who were also consumers. They also provided new subsistence commodities like coffee, cacao, beef, and tropical fruits, which were required in growing amounts by the markets of industrialized societies. Thus, the same industrial progress that multiplied the factories in countries central to the system, also stimulated expansion of commercial agriculture, herding, and the extraction of forest products and minerals in peripheral countries.

Imperialistic implantation occurred in three stages, which reflect changes in methods and goals during evolution of the systems of external exploitation. The first stage was characterized by the export of manufactured goods and the acquisition of exclusive sources of raw materials or of captive markets, either by imposition of colonial rule or the institution of neocolonial relations that functionally replaced the earlier mercantile formations. The second stage was marked by fusion of businesses into large monopolies controlled by financial agencies, which operated principally through exportation of capital, both in the form of equipment for modernization of production and of monetary loans to governments. This development intensified the exploitation of peoples occupying a subordinate position in the system because it was furthered by the instruments of industrialization themselves in the form of railroads, ports, modern communication systems, and specialized types of machinery. Subordination to the influence of a great power was also intensified by the fact that, paradoxically, the dependent nations were obliged to pay for the equipment that served principally to make them more efficient providers of the raw materials required by industrialized nations.

In the third stage, subsidiaries of the great monopolistic corporations were installed in the dependent countries to exploit the internal market, and thus to drain off more effectively the capital generated in the poor countries for the enrichment of the wealthy ones. As a result of diffusion of the industrial technology, an evolutionary acceleration appears to have occurred during this last step. Behaving as a form of historical incorporation, however, this industrialization did not generate the progressive effects that had been produced in self-industrialized nations. Instead, it led to increased dependence and to a process of reflexive modernization, which created such profound deformations that the nations involved were condemned to backwardness and want. Under these conditions, which offered no possibilities for integration into the modernized productive system, the expanding populations remained marginal. Nor could education reach the level required to master the scientific principles of the new productive technology. There was even less prospect of creating an autonomous elite committed to ending the external exploitation and to reforming the archaic social order.

Although initiated more than two centuries ago, the civilizational processes stemming from the Industrial Revolution continue to unfold. It has not yet realized its full potential even in the areas where it first began. A long range view makes it evident that it has represented both a progressive advance and a dissociative eruption. It contains sufficient energy to destroy or render obsolete old ways of life. Conditioned by the profit-making character of the businesses it generates, however, and convulsed by an increasing rate of renovation, it lacks the capacity to promote the industrialization of new areas, or to secure peace, stability, well being, and liberty for the populations it has integrated into a single economic system.

In the central areas, the Industrial Revolution has accelerated social evolution, creating a new type of society that is qualitatively distinct from earlier ones. In peripheral areas, where it acts reflexively or by means of historical incorporation, it has produced equally great transformations, but in so doing has generated dissociative processes of growing intensity. As with earlier technological revolutions, autonomous industrialization has reorganized relations between peoples, favoring the most advanced, and failing to establish mechanisms for the transition from traditional ways of life, now archaic, to new ones. As a consequence, it has created an international configuration polarized around the pioneer industrial nations, which display extreme hostility to the development of other peoples.

After the *early model of industrial development* was established in England (1750–1800), France (1800–1850), and the United States of America (1840–1890), these three countries divided up the world into regions for exploitation or subordination, within which only a limited and dependent kind of development henceforth became possible. Other colonial powers like Spain, Portugal, Holland, and Russia, which had lagged in industrialization, perforce took second place to the new centers of domination.

The first successful breach in this circle of domination was made by three countries representing the *late model of industrial development:* Germany (1850–1914), Japan (1900–1920), and Italy (1920–1940). All attained this new state through the formulation and execution of autonomous development projects. These were directed principally by the national government, which was motivated by considerations of national security and military might, and which resorted to heterodox procedures like management of the economy and a guarantee of full employment—in extreme contrast to the free exchange and free trade principles that ruled the pioneer industrialized nations. Implemented by politico-military leaders in association with business plutocracies, these new procedures inevitably provoked opposition from the previously industrialized nations. The result was a series of local and world wars to force a redistribution of the areas of domination and the recognition of an equal status for the new industrial powers. As a consequence, the Germans acquired colonial possessions in Africa and later in Asia; the Japanese conquered areas of former Russian domination and invaded Manchuria; and the Italians seized control over large portions of northern Africa.

These conflicts led to the emergence of two new patterns of autonomous industrial development, revolutionary socialism, which took shape as a separate formation, and recent capitalistic development, which appeared in marginal areas like Scandinavia (1900–1920), or in dependent regions like Canada (1900–1920) and Australia (1930–1950). In the latter two countries, the change resulted from modifications in commercial relations with more highly industrialized countries during periods of war or crisis. Under normal conditions, such relations do not lead to autonomous progress because their character is intrinsically exploitative. During a wartime emergency, however, dependent nations are able to export more than they import, and consequently to accumulate foreign exchange. Above all, they are stimulated to a voluntary exploitation of their own sources of wealth, permitting realization of potentialities for progress that had formerly been denied. After the international conflict ends, this economic strengthening may be sufficiently advanced to permit negotiation for new kinds of economic interaction, which favor preservation of national economic interests and thus permit further autonomous development.

As can be seen, the impact of the Industrial Revolution has been expressed in different ways, depending on whether it was experienced directly or indirectly. In the former case, modern societies were created; in the latter, underdeveloped nations. Both are products of the same renovating forces, which on the one hand realized their potentialities through evolutionary acceleration, and on the other were limited externally by imperialistic exploitation and internally by a constrictive oligarchy, so that expression took the form of historical incorporation. The condition of underdevelopment thus does not represent simple retardation, or an archaic type of society. On the contrary, it constitutes a necessary sequel to the renovating forces of the Industrial Revolution, which generated two simultaneous products: industrial centers with highly developed technological economies, and Neo-Colonial nations structured less to take care of their own needs than to provide goods and services for the industrial centers. The colonial populations, degraded by deculturation or by deterioration of their traditional economy, slip back from levels of technological development previously achieved, and become transformed into a labor force utilized in the most primitive way, namely as human fuel for the productive process.

Underdevelopment does not represent a crisis in growth, therefore, but rather a trauma that has affected societies subordinated to the industrial centers. Social tensions have been aggravated to an extreme degree by addition of demographic explosion and accelerated chaotic urbanization, which cannot be resolved or even moderated by export of the excess population as Europe was able to do under similar circumstances. Self-correcting forces cannot be generated internally because control rests outside the affected society, and because the potentialities of the industrial technology are only applied in the areas and within the limits required to make the peripheral economies more efficient in their traditional role. In other words, only incomplete and deformed kinds of modernization are permitted and these deepen the dependence. Societies thus created can never achieve an autonomous and self-sustaining economy capable of exploiting its own growth potential because of the fact that they constitute functional parts of other economies in an interacting and self-perpetuating system.

Furthermore, underdeveloped nations are not simply backward, they are also the despoiled nations of history, having been impoverished by pillage of their accumulated treasure and of the fruits of labor of their people. To all these handicaps can be added deformation of the ruling class which, placed at the service of foreign exploitation, becomes incapable of innovative and competitive action. Because of these circumstances, relative backwardness is not a transitional stage between archaic and modern forms of society, but a structural condition that inhibits progress.

The non-industrialized nations of the modern world, therefore, are not survivals or contemporary examples of an earlier stage passed through by the developed countries. On the contrary, they are the result of a process of historical incorporation that exploits them in order to accelerate the development of other areas. Tensions between these underdeveloped societies and the imperialistic centers that benefit from their retardation have grown to major proportions in recent times, becoming increasingly bitter as aspirations for industrial goods become more general, as the leadership of the underdeveloped countries begins to realize that the system cannot lead to autonomous development, and as the exploited populations are integrated into new national ethnos able to fight for emancipation.

A new historical movement is forming in which prosperous and powerful peoples are aligned on one side and underdeveloped peoples on the other. The latter are split into those who identify with the existing system because they know how to profit from it, and those who are opposed to the system because they perceive that their backward condition is unnecessary. Struggles for emancipation from the colonial yoke and internal conflicts for structural reorganization are thus exploding in underdeveloped societies. Since these societies, as providers of raw materials, as absorbers of goods and services, and as producers of foreign profits, are indispensable to the functioning and perpetuation of the capitalist order, their aspirations for autonomy and their internal revolutionary tensions threaten the system itself. Because they attack the economic foundation, which is based on a division of functions between prosperous and impoverished peoples, they will force reorganization not only of the social system but of the whole civilization. By the end of World War I, struggles for political emancipation in colonial areas and for developmental autonomy in Neo-Colonial areas had become strong enough to constitute a new civilizational process, leading in turn to the emergence of new sociocultural formations.

At this point, it is necessary to establish a clear distinction between backward peoples and underdeveloped peoples. The former correspond to the marginal contingents not influenced by some (or all) of the technological revolutions that have shaped the modern world. Examples include the pre-agricultural tribes and Undifferentiated Horticultural Villages that still survive in remote areas. In contrast to this archaic and isolated condition, underdeveloped peoples are those who have been integrated into the world economic system by processes of historical incorporation, and who as they achieve ethnic maturation have become increasingly aware of the spoliative nature of their external relations and the reactionary character of their traditional ruling classes.

Underdeveloped nations can be classified into four large cultural historical configurations, which equate with their specific processes of ethnic formation, and which are responsible for the problems of development now facing their populations. The first of these is the *Emerging Peoples*, who are advancing at the present time from a tribal to a national condition under the influence of processes of historical incorporation that tend to convert them into Neo-Colonial areas. Such peoples exist principally in tropical Africa, and were until recently (or still remain) under English, French, Belgian, Portuguese, or other colonial domination. Their national economies are operated by foreign enclaves implanted like cysts into their territories, and which take the form of mining enterprises (Congo, Zambia, Rhodesia, Nigeria, Katanga, and Cameroon), large tropical export plantations (Liberia, Ghana, Nigeria, Guinea, Somali, Kenya, Sudan, Tanzania, Angola, and Mozambique), or areas of pastoral or forest product exploitation.

Second are the *New Peoples,* all of whom are located in Latin America, and who represent intrusive by-products of European slavistic colonialism. The combination of profoundly diversified ethnic groups—indigenous, Negro, and European—through racial mixture and acculturation has given rise to new ethnic likenesses. Detribalization and compulsory deculturation destroyed most of the original cultural heritage, but only those new cultural elements could be adopted that were compatible with the requirements of the colonial system. Today such nations are not only unhampered by conservatism in any form, but to a certain degree are predisposed toward change since their only hope for the future lies in their integration into the ways of life of modern industrial societies. This is the case with Brazil, Venezuela, Colombia, and the Antilles, where European-Negro mixture predominates. It is also true of Chile, Paraguay, Uruguay, Argentina, and of certain countries in Central America, where European-indigenous mixture is the prevalent form. (Uruguay and Argentina were later modified by the avalanche of European immigrants who arrived after independence.) None of the representatives of this configuration has achieved fully developed industrialization; all can be categorized as dependent areas of a Neo-Colonial character.

The third configuration is that of the *Witness Peoples,* which have resulted from the impact of European expansion during the Mercantile and Industrial Revolutions on ancient civilizations like the Moslem, Indian, Chinese, Korean, Indochinese, Peruvian, and Mexican ones. All have suffered profound traumatizations from which they are only now beginning to recover during the course of integration into industrial civilization. Japan took the capitalist route and, more recently, China and North Korea have taken the socialist route. The rest have retained underdeveloped Neo-Colonial economies, except for Mexico, Egypt, and Algeria, which are now emerging into a new formation: the Nationalistic Modernizing States.

The fourth configuration corresponds to the *Transplanted Peoples,* and comprises European populations that were dislodged, prinicipally from rural areas, and relocated overseas as a consequence of the civilizational processes that shaped the Capitalistic Mercantile and Imperialistic Industrial formations. As discontinuous extensions of European culture, these peoples carried forward the technological renovation and institutional reorganization that had been taking place at home. For this reason, and also because of the less exploitative character of the domination to which they were subjected, greater opportunities have existed for their integration into modern industrial civilization. The United States, Canada, Australia, and New Zealand are good examples. After a transformation of their earlier ethnos as a result of their encouragement of mass immigration, Argentina and Uruguay also entered this category. They did so at a less-developed level, however, because of retention of an oligarchical institutional organization based on monopoly of land, which was one of the last elements of their Iberian salvationistic heritage. Also among the Transplanted Peoples, although less typical, are the Caucasoid nuclei in South Africa, Rhodesia, Kenya, and Israel. They represent European intrusions into foreign populations, which have neither been absorbed by miscegenation nor decimated. Because of their artificial character, all of these nations will probably undergo profound ethnic transformations, and with maturation of a new national ethnos, these unassimilable intrusions will sooner or later tend to be repelled.

Socialistic Expansion

After World War I, the renovating forces of the Industrial Revolution gave rise to a new civilizational process responsible for the appearance of socialistic formations. These emerged from the action of three kinds of tensions, all generated or intensified by industrialization, and all irreducible within the context of the Imperialistic Industrial and Neo-Colonial formations.

The first of these were tensions between the Imperialistic Industrial Powers themselves, which led to successive wars to partition the colonial cake, and finally to world-wide conflagrations that severely weakened the mechanisms for preservation of the capitalistic system. The second type of tensions arose between the industrialized nations and their areas of exploitation. The latter areas, condemned to backwardness by the exploitative nature of their reciprocal relations, embarked on wars of independence that

placed the whole social order on trial and led to profound structural reforms. In the third category were internal tensions, which stemmed from
the internal bifurcation of both dominant and dependent societies into opposing forces, one composed of the managerial classes fighting to maintain
the *status quo* and to secure as large a proportion of the profits as possible,
and the other composed of the lower classes constantly striving to raise their
level of consumption and to improve their living and working conditions.

Varying combinations of these three kinds of tensions lead to two basic
processes for social restructuring. One is evolutionary and results from the
accumulation of institutional changes that ultimately modify the capitalistic regime sufficiently to create a new formation, the *Socialistic Evolutionary Nations*. The other is revolutionary, led by political forces that inten-
tionally rupture obstacles to autonomous industrial development and shape
societies into two other new formations, *Socialistic Revolutionary Nations*
and *Nationalistic Modernizing States*.

In constructing the theoretical model for Socialistic Evolutionary formations, we had in mind several highly industrialized nations that have taken
a course divergent both from Imperialistic Industrial structures and from
Socialistic Revolutionary ones. The most mature examples are the Scandinavian countries, which have combined certain collectivistic measures
for production, consumption, and state responsibility for social welfare,
with the preservation in other sectors of private enterprise for the pursuit
of profits, and in association with liberal political institutions. A less mature
form exists in England which, impoverished by the last war, dispossessed
of its principal colonies, and subordinated to the North American economy,
found it necessary for its own survival to adopt democratizing structural
reforms and a collectivistic reorganization of the national economy. Certain
revolutionary movements in France and Italy also suggest a progressive
evolution toward socialism, invalidating the rule that this must occur by
passage through a "dictatorship of the proletariat" and by recourse to a
single party system. These examples also cast doubt on the prior necessity
for nationalization of the means of production. Austria too appears to be
heading toward this formation through the combination of spontaneous
structural changes with deliberate political reorganization.

Some of the theorists who extol the free market economy most highly
have attempted to use such instances to demonstrate the viability of the
capitalistic system and its capacity for evolutionary renovation. In their

view, spontaneous socialization is occurring in the form of expanding popular ownership of businesses and an increasingly egalitarian distribution of the fruits of human labor, along with democratization of social and political institutions. Their opposition to socialism is based essentially on a denial of the desirability for rational intervention in the economic, political, or social structure. They are confident that spontaneously interacting social and economic forces, controlled informally by the profit system and the demands of the open market, will produce the best results by allowing progressive maturation of the potentialities for abundance and liberty that are inherent in modern technology.

Although the neo-capitalistic theorists appear to be correct in recognizing a spontaneous tendency toward socialism, the reasons for its occurrence are certainly not the ones that they cite. The fundamental characteristic of evolutionary socialism, according to Schumpeter (1951, 1956), is the fact that it does not emerge through maturation of the capitalist system, but results instead from the attenuation of its crucial features which, at a certain stage, creates a counterfeit capitalistic configuration tending toward socialism. In fact, the capitalistic industrial system, after establishing a regime of contractual rationalization, of spontaneity, of private domain, and of economic liberalism, began not only to restore old protective regulations but to create new ones. The generalization of such measures inevitably causes obsolescence of the system. Nor are these measures voluntary concessions to the salaried masses; instead, they are the price for survival in the face of the insurrections, strikes, and class struggles that have convulsed capitalistic societies ever since the last quarter of the past century. These movements have obliged governments to restrain their most flagrant abuses, which has been done by regulating the working conditions of minors and women, by permitting labor the freedom to organize and the right to strike, by limiting the length of the work day, by fixing minimum salaries, and by establishing services for the prediction and prevention of unemployment.

Through such measures, capitalistic governments began to assume increasing social responsibilities toward the labor force, thus raising the cost of social services and requiring investment of growing portions of the national income. These procedures have led to new systems for the distribution of national revenue, which have further intensified state intervention and culminated in making the government primarily responsible for the fate of business. Under these circumstances, business itself begins to welcome state protection in the form of direct or indirect subsidies to industry and agriculture. In the industrial capitalistic nations where this process has operated most intensively, the free enterprise system has entered a new dimension that makes survival of the regime depend, paradoxically, on its increasing decomposition. The state has begun to change from a force subordinate to privatistic interests into a renovating power, motivated by the necessity of maintaining a no-longer viable economy in order to ensure political stability and high levels of employment, and of manipulating inflation and deflation in order to prevent economic recession.

This new economic policy, which arose through the need to reduce dangerously revolutionary tensions between management and labor, matured into economic planning, which was also required to deal with local and general crises, and to mobilize the economy for war. Progression of this unwanted but inevitable government intervention has culminated by affecting the conditions essential to functioning of the capitalist system, especially since a concomitant restructuring of the external economy has been imposed by emergence to independence of former colonial domains and by competition with more powerful capitalist and socialist structures. At a certain point in the process, the economic system becomes so profoundly altered that it more closely resembles the theoretical model of socialism than the original capitalist model. The whole economy comes to be regulated principally by the state, which establishes the limits between public and private sectors, and which is more concerned with social goals than with the free interaction of businesses in search of higher profits.

In highly industrialized capitalist societies, socialistic tendencies tend to be strengthened by additional reorganizing forces, which are based less on politico-institutional factors than on deeper processes of structural renovation. Among these forces is a drastic reduction in the number of people devoted to agricultural work, accompanied by a propensity to erase millennia-old urban-rural distinctions. England at present has under 5 percent of her working population occupied in agriculture; the United States figure is under 10 percent (United Nations, 1964b). The latter case is especially significant, because it represents the most productive agricultural economy in the world. As a consequence of similar fusions of agriculture with industry, other industrialized nations with highly mechanized agriculture also show the same tendency, as well as a similar minimization of distinctions between rural and urban ways of life. In fact, the structural maturity of a society can be measured by the index attained in this fusion and in its basic indicator, which is the reduced frequency of agricultural labor in the working population.

Another structural renovation has led the majority of the labor force released from agriculture, not into industry, but instead into numerous new categories of services (social, educational, commercial, bureaucratic, recreational, etc.), which have shown a remarkable capacity to absorb workers. In France between 1850 and 1950, the proportion of workers in industry rose from about 30 percent to 40 percent, while this third sector (services) grew from 16 percent to 30 percent. In the United States between 1870 and 1950, the increases were from 22.4 to 40.2 percent and from 19.0 to 44.4 percent, respectively. The "white collar" category in the United States absorbed 10.6 million new workers between 1948 and 1963, while rural wage earners increased by only 1.6 million. The predominant occupational category in industrialized societies thus tends to be salaried office employees and university graduates, rather than factory workers (Clark, 1957; Fourastié, 1960). Expansion of this third sector does not imply a greater economic independence for the individual, however, since businesses tend to agglutinate into increasingly larger entities with the result that the ratio of wage earners to proprietors and self-employed (farmers, professionals, etc.) constantly increases.

These tendencies have become accentuated during the past decade with the appearance of electronic technology and the first steps toward automation of the productive system. It is to be expected that these innovations will be reflected on the social level by a strengthening of socialistic tendencies, because they permit production of such extraordinarily large amounts of goods that the need to work for a living may become obsolete. Wiener, who has discussed the probable consequences of automation, has expressed concern for the disruptive effects that can result; he has also pointed out that "the answer, of course, is to have a society based on human values other than buying or selling" (1948, p. 28). This can take place, however, only in the course of a new civilizational process.

An alternative path of post-capitalist evolution is revolutionary socialism, which has developed in the Soviet Union, the socialist republics of eastern Europe, China, North Korea, North Vietnam, and Cuba. The principal characteristic of this sociocultural formation is its rationality as manifested in plans for the reform of human societies and the adoption of

these plans through revolution. A theoretical model of planned social transformation for salaried workers, especially those in factories, was fore-
shadowed in the early socialist doctrines, particularly Marxism. These also
defined a strategy that for the first time offered to the subordinate classes
prospects for the realization of old aspirations for a complete reorganization
of the basis of social life. According to Marxist theory, the working class
is historically destined to be the moving force of a social revolution that
will eliminate all forms of despoilment and alienation through the abolition of private ownership of the means of production and the resultant
eradication of class structure and mechanisms of state oppression.

A special feature of the theoretical model of Marxist socialism is its dual
character, in which the anticipation of a new stage of human evolution is
combined with an intentional project for the reorganization of society along
majority interests. The first aspect follows from the conception of its for-
mulators that socialism represents a new sociocultural formation, a natural
and necessary stage in the evolution of capitalist societies. The second aspect
derives from the assumption that this transformation is not inevitable, and
that it consequently requires development of a strategy, first for winning
power, and subsequently for implanting the new system. Both aspects
create the expectation that socialistic formations will emerge only after
profound convulsions of a revolutionary character, and via transitional
regimes that take the form of "dictatorships of the proletariat."

This expectation has not been fulfilled, however, by the mature industrialized societies, which have the largest and most awakened proletariats.
Nor has it been provoked, as the Marxist theorists predicted, either by
exhaustion of the potentialities of the capitalist regime, or as a consequence
of cyclic crises or of growing impoverishment of the working masses. Only
one intentional program of social reorganization has been instigated, and
this was in a marginal area with only incipient capitalism and industrialization: we refer to the Russian socialist revolution of 1917. This has been
followed by several other social revolutions, all of them provoked primarily
by anti-oligarchical and anti-imperialist tensions which, except in the case
of Cuba, have been released in the course of world wars.

Just as the mercantile and industrial capitalistic formations have taken
distinct historical forms that may occasionally conflict with one another,
so have the socialistic formations assumed diverse and markedly nationalistic shapes likely to find themselves in opposition. A case in point is the

Sino-Soviet disagreement. Nevertheless, all examples of Socialistic Revolutionary organization are variations of the model crystallized in the Soviet Union after 1917; they are authoritarian regimes of rational intervention in all aspects of social life, characterized by overall planning and total mobilization of energies to eradicate archaic social structures and install new ways of life and work. Even the most divergent socialist patterns, like those of Jugoslavia, Cuba, and China, do not depart basically from this model. Furthermore, none of them, not even the oldest, claims to represent the definitive form that is sought. All identify themselves as transitional states dedicated to the acceleration both of technological-industrial progress and of social and ideological restructuring, in order to provide a foundation for the establishment of future communist societies. As a consequence, all fall into a single sociocultural formation, the Socialistic Revolutionary Nations, which is characterized by "dictatorship of the proletariat" as an instrument for the mobilization of resources and energies in order to accelerate compulsory socialization of the means of production. The objective is the creation of a new type of industrial economy in which economic oppression, social inequality, and the opposition both between rural and urban, and between physical and intellectual types of work will become obsolete.

Implementation of this model in Russia was a severe challenge because it constituted the first voluntary attempt at rational restructuring of a whole society from its foundations. An effort was made to fulfill ancient humanistic aspirations within a rigid economic framework that made prosperity dependent on productive capacity, and well-being dependent on a delicate equilibrium between the necessity for a growing investment in production and the desire to increase popular consumption. Three types of measures were adopted. First, a new power structure was created by elimination of the former ruling class and the recruitment and training of a new technocratic group. Second, a new socio-economic system was established that had the capacity to mobilize both the capital obtained by appropriation of productive goods and the whole national labor force for a continuing effort to expand heavy industry; and this could be accomplished only by rigorous control of all factors able to affect the program and by adoption of overall governmental planning. Third, external and internal hostility to this social experiment required the arousal of national energies for self-defense and the diversion of an appreciable portion of resources to military ends. This unfavorable atmosphere limited the extent to which the Soviet socialist project could reduce class differences and implant a popular democracy. It explains the fact that in spite of the efforts expended and the progress achieved, all socialist societies retain both class stratifications that differentiate urban wage earners from the peasantry, and social distinctions that favor the incumbent bureaucracy. In addition, statism has survived and been strengthened—contrary to the expectations of the theorists—giving rise to various forms of bureaucratic party despotism.

These drawbacks seem to be offset only by the scope of the educational system, which permits the selection of new talent from the whole population, and by the expectation that the combination of this democratic basis for education with a state system of merit promotion will equalize opportunities for social ascent in each new generation. Socialistic Revolutionary societies appear to rely on these measures to minimize the risks of stagnation and despotism that overcame the Theocratic Irrigation formations, which were also based on state ownership of the means of production and directed by technocracies that tended to become hereditary, rigid, and despotic. Socialist societies also depend on such measures to counteract two serious additional threats. One stems from the Russian and Chinese heritage of despotic traditions from the periods of Mongoloid and Manchu domination experienced by both. The other derives from the absence of a history of liberal democratic traditions in these two societies, and makes it necessary for them to undertake programs of political mobilization and ideological maturation to prepare their populations for self-government, along with programs for industrialization and the corresponding social restructuring. In the Chinese model of revolutionary socialism, the confrontation of these threats appears to be taking a bolder form. Economic stimuli and the traditional emphasis on military hierarchies and technocratic direction have been abandoned and the non-metropolitan population has been restructured into rural-urban communes. Above all there has been an ideological mobilization of the entire population for the renovation of Chinese civilization via a "cultural revolution."

The failure of Socialistic Revolutionary movements in the most industrialized societies can be explained primarily by the capacity of such structures to satisfy the basic material aspirations of their metropolitan populations. This has been possible because of the acceleration of technological progress during the Industrial Revolution, which permitted capitalist enterprises to maintain their profit rates in spite of a constant increase in labor cost. It is also partly explainable, however, by the repression exercised in imperialistic states against reorganizational impulses originating among the lower classes. This repression is manifested in a number of ways, among them: (1) encouragement of massive emigrations, and decimation in warfare, both of which also diminished social tensions in the earliest industrialized areas; (2) acquisition of supplementary wealth through colonial exploration; (3) institutionalization of class conflicts, especially by the creation of trade unions which, instead of maturing the worker's consciousness of the historic role foretold for him, have diverted a large part of the revolutionary impetus into economic gain; (4) ideological indoctrination incorporating antisocialist religious propaganda; (5) development of protectionist social legislation, and multiplication of social services that improve the conditions of life among the lower classes; (6) police and military repression of socialist-revolutionary working class movements; and (7) creation of political terrorist regimes. The latter received extreme expression in Fascism and Nazism, both movements devoted primarily to frustration of the insurrections that threatened to lead Italy and Germany into socialism.

Paradoxically, the Soviet experiment, and especially the distorted image of it that has been diffused, exercised a restraining influence on socialist movements of a more utopian inspiration. This experiment demonstrated that a revolutionary transition to socialism does not automatically follow collectivization of the means of production. On the contrary, its achievement requires a continuing political effort, involving great strengthening of the power of the state and enormous sacrifices on the part of the population. The Soviet example has further shown that socialism does not eliminate either division of labor and the resultant hierarchy of functions, or the salaried regime and a monetary economy.

The hostility exhibited by capitalist nations during the crucial period in its efforts toward industrialization reinforced other arguments to compel the USSR to adopt stringent measures for popular mobilization and moral compulsion. Being based on patriotic and personal values, these measures strengthened nationalism and inevitably moderated enthusiasm for the international communist movement. Furthermore, after 1935 the socialist and communist parties themselves became more concerned with co-participation in governmental organs, via parliamentary tactics and a united front, than with a direct conquest of power. This new orientation, along with a tendency to institutionalize class tensions through the expansion of labor unions, led to a growing bureaucratization of these two fronts of the revolutionary movement. In the process, both were transformed into cogs in the institutional machine with the function of regulating and controlling the working masses, and as a result, of consolidating capitalism itself. Leftist parties consequently began to support evolutionary socialism as a more desirable alternative to the capitalist system, and to concentrate their efforts on campaigns to force redistribution of the fruits of technological progress, rather than on the intentional reorganization of society as a whole.

There is nothing to indicate that the existing varieties of revolutionary and evolutionary socialism exhaust the possibilities for socialistic organization; on the contrary, technological innovations, structural reorganizations, and institutional renovations developed during recent decades, both in the advanced capitalist societies and in underdeveloped areas, provide new opportunities for social organization along socialistic principles. One of these tendencies is evident in a few backward nations that are fighting for economic and political autonomy in a world divided into capitalist and socialist camps, and which are searching for a new structural model that will provide them with opportunities for industrialization and development. These are the Nationalistic Modernizing States, which are based on structural principles of primarily socialist inspiration such as popular mobilization for developmental efforts, state interventionism and partial economic planning, and other measures favoring public enterprise. They are also based on a vigorous anti-oligarchical reformism, which is expressed in agrarian reform programs for the integration of marginal groups into the national economy and in the creation of a broad middle segment of small proprietors. Finally, they cultivate nationalism as a clearly anti-imperialistic ideology conducive to wars of emancipation, as a justification for economic development along independent lines, and as the expression of a national ethos mature enough to take pride in its image and prepared to assume control over its destiny. Examples of this formation are provided by the Mexico of Cardenas, the Turkey of Mustafa Kemal, and by present-day Egypt and Algeria, along with other nations of the "Third World." All have attempted to overcome underdevelopment by measures that are comparable to those adopted by socialist countries, but which are much less radical and much less effective in bringing about autonomous industrialization.

The fact that all Nationalistic Modernizing formations have been produced by revolutionary movements is indicative of the level of resistance offered by colonial and oligarchical interests to any kind of structural reform. It also reveals the weight of opposition to exposure of the spurious nature of such values as Eurocentrism, racism, and anti-tropicalism, whose real function is to explain and justify backwardness. The intermediate position taken by Nationalistic Modernizing formations between capitalist and radical socialist solutions is to some extent a reflection of the ideological posture of their revolutionary leadership. It also expresses the conditions of economic retardation and structural deformation that result from the internal oligarchical constrictions and external exploitation of which they have been long-term victims, and which must be superseded. Finally, it indicates the power of Imperialistic Industrial formations to maintain the *status quo,* which was sufficient to force societies such as Turkey and Mexico to turn back from this path, and to prevent many others from electing to adopt it.

Quantification of differences in the efficiency of renovative action exhibited by Socialistic Revolutionary Nations as compared to Nationalistic Modernizing ones, demonstrates that the former have a considerably greater capacity to promote industrial acceleration. The USSR laid the foundation of its industrial system between 1930 and 1940, and China between 1955 and 1965, through unprecedented rates of increase in their gross national products. This capacity for evolutionary acceleration has made the socialist revolutionary course particularly attractive for other underdeveloped nations facing similar problems and possessing similar or inferior pre-existing socio-economic conditions, in terms both of the size of their marginal populations and of the technological retardation of their productive systems. Perpetuation of their integration within the international imperialist system implies for these nations an acceptance of their condemnation to backwardness, and the abandonment of hope for improvement in the foreseeable future, since mature industrial capitalist economies progress at a much faster rate than underdeveloped ones.

A concrete example of this situation is provided by Brazil, which today has a population of 85 million and enormous natural resources, but which nevertheless faces grave problems of development. Until recently, Brazil had one of the highest rates of economic growth among underdeveloped nations; namely, a 2.8 percent per capita annual increase in its gross national product between 1955 and 1960. At this rate, however, it would take Brazil 132 years to reach the 1966 level of per capita income and productivity of the United States. Even under the Soviet rate of 6.4 percent per capita per year (maintained between 1950 and 1960), Brazil could not catch up with the United States for 40 years (Kuznets, 1964).[3]

Socialistic Revolutionary Nations and Socialistic Evolutionary Nations have strongly contrasting ideological profiles. The former are imbued with egalitarian ideas and a utopian mystique; the latter, with liberal values and pessimistic realism. Each has little or no appreciation of the values cultivated by the other. Because the Socialistic Evolutionary Nations are emerging from advanced industrial capitalist structures, they preserve the notions of spontaneity intrinsic to the ancestral system, thus making it extremely difficult for them to plan a rational reorganization of society. As a result, they have nothing comparable to the ideological profile of Socialistic Revolutionary Nations, which attempt to rationalize themselves in terms of a libertarian mystique and as the way of progress for retarded societies. On the contrary, they can even be said to be characterized by an aversion to ideological formulations in general. This does not imply an absence of ideology, however, since concealment of its true function, the perpetuation of the existing social order, also constitutes an ideology. In such an atmosphere the thinkers are compelled to assume a passive role as observers of the "spontaneous action of natural forces," or to devote themselves to the task of persuading society that "free" interaction between the agents of change will lead to the best results. In the past, Calvinist ideology provided a divine justification for such an attitude; today, it is merely "wishful thinking."

This theoretical aridity contrasts strikingly with the creativity and daring manifested by the early spokesmen for capitalism. Then, a multiplicity of philosophers devoted themselves to retracing the course of man and society, and in so doing created the theoretical foundations of a modern political

---

[3] The aforementioned figures were compiled by the author who, with the help of a mathematician, calculated the Brazilian foreseeable rate of development under the capitalistic average and socialistic rates, using data derived from a United Nations study (1964a) and Kuznets (1964).

ideology. Today one searches in vain for the emulators of those old humanists. Could it be that the Socialistic Evolutionary model is so unviable and so fragile in its foundations as to incite no enthusiasm? Is it a true sociocultural formation, or is it merely a transition between deteriorating capitalism and new forms not yet clearly recognizable? These questions have considerable importance because civilizations can develop only when they are able to imbue a sense of mission in their populations that offers a higher destiny than mere existence (Linton, 1936). This capacity for ideological seduction permitted the great civilizations of the past to mobilize their populations for imperial expansion, for creation of an integrated macroethnos, or for production to enrich the dominant minority. When this characteristic is absent, the integrative function tends either to become extremely despotic or to be diluted, as occurs in feudalized societies, with the result that the whole culture is mediocratized, although people are able to live more tranquilly, and probably enjoy better and more abundant food.

Universal

Civilization

The Thermonuclear Revolution and Future Societies

Accelerative impulses can be observed during the course of every technological revolution. Progressive spurts occurred a number of times during the Industrial Revolution; for example, following the introduction of steam turbines, electric motors, and internal combustion engines; after the substitution of steel for iron in industrial uses; after the appearance of machine tools (lathe, grinder, milling machine, etc.); with the development of the chemical industry; and with the generalized use of electric apparatus. In spite of the resulting significant changes in the productive process and ways of life of mankind, however, the fact that new sociocultural formations did not emerge is justification for not recognizing such accelerations as separate technological revolutions.

The advent of a modern scientific technology based on thermonuclear and electronic developments has already led to prodigious transformations in the productive system, and is likely to provoke even more radical modifications in the future. Are we to view this as just another cyclical acceleration? Or should it be classified as a new technological revolution? The magnitude of the progress already achieved and its eruptive character both suggest that a revolution is indeed involved. After a period of slack between the final decade of the past century and the third decade of this one, scientific technological creativity has resumed growth in an extraordinary way (Lilley, 1948). Such a profusion of innovations enhancing man's capacity for action, thought, organization, and planning has accumulated since the last world war as to indicate that a new technological revolution is in fact taking shape.

If this is true, we are as yet only on the threshhold of this new revolution, and its renovative impact can barely be distinguished at the present time from those effects still stemming from the Industrial Revolution. Our times can be compared with the first quarter of the 19th century in England when the Industrial Revolution was molding a new and still nebulous formation. A comparison of the mature fruits of the Industrial Revolution with those initial sprouts highlights their primitive and rudimentary nature. They nevertheless contained the potentialities of all future developments. In like manner, the current accumulation of advances in basic science and their multiplicity of technological applications are a mere preview of things to come in the next few decades.

The impact of modern scientific technology has already made itself felt in the life of the average man, principally through a flood of new materials, new types of automatic machine tools, and revolutionary methods of mass communication. It has fantastically increased the acuity of human senses and wrought unimagined contractions of space and extensions of time. The most critical effects are concentrated, however, in military technology, which now holds absolute power for the eradication of life on earth. Even so, the prospects of this new technology for making available prodigious resources of energy, and for creating limitless abundance in goods and services, remain little more than expectations. As these expectations become fulfilled, they will initiate a new movement to eliminate the economy of scarcity and to substitute an economy of abundance. In the process, all existing forms of social stratification will be altered, and division of society into economic classes will fade and finally disappear. This trend will be resisted by privatist interests with the desperate vigor characteristic of a struggle for survival, because their privileges depend upon the existence of social inequality. It is to be expected that this conflict will reach catastrophic dimensions when the new economy achieves a greater maturity, since it erupted under the mere theoretical possibility of establishing equality and abundance raised by the civilizational process that crystallized the first socialist formations.

In short, it is evident that a new civilizational process of universal scope is unfolding at an accelerated rate. It is governed by the fundamental principle underlying sociocultural evolution, which assigns primary motive power to major improvements in the productive process. It is one thing to create a working prototype of a polished ax, a plow, a sailboat, an automobile, or a television set, and another to make these available by the millions. The Thermonuclear Revolution will consequently make itself felt as a new force for the molding of history only when all the prodigious paraphernalia now being imagined or planned have actually been put into modern industrial use.

This emerging wave of technological innovations and sociocultural concomitants can justifiably be designated as the Thermonuclear Revolution not only because of the overriding importance of the energy factor in cultural evolution, but also because of the impact on humanity of the atomic competition between the United States and the Soviet Union that has existed since the end of World War II. This competition has led to an unparalleled reallocation of financial and human resources. Today, the United States applies some 75 percent of its budget to defense ($84 billion in 1966); more than $897 billion have been spent since 1946. It maintains an army of six million soldiers (e.g., NATO, SEATO) dispersed over the world, as well as 350,000 scientists and technicians representing some 900 different specialties (de Carlo, 1964). Since the Soviet and Chinese military investments are probably comparable, it is evident that we are faced with a new decisive situation in terms both of its magnitude and of its capacity to affect human society. Although only a portion of this fantastic mobilization of resources involves nuclear technology (future conflicts are envisioned more in terms of chemical-biological warfare than as atomic contests), thermonuclear competition and the resulting fear of total destruction have initiated the technological revolution and provoked the extraordinary acceleration that we are experiencing today (Kahn, 1962; Halperin, 1965, 1967).

Even in these early stages, the Thermonuclear Revolution has placed at the disposal of the most advanced societies fantastic amounts of destructive, constructive, and constrictive power. This can lead man either to a regime of plenty and equality, or to a sociocultural and even biological deterioration more pronounced than in any previous regression. Whatever man's destiny, he must pass through this stage, and he will be indelibly marked by his passage. During the transition, it is conceivable that the evolutionary process may cease to be a spontaneous historical movement, propelled by accumulation of advances in methods of dealing with nature and the "natural" effects of these advances on human society, and will become instead a rational and directed process. If so, the major challenge facing the most advanced societies today will be to regulate the process of change provoked by scientific-technological development, so as to determine its rate and to establish the manner in which it will exert its effects on the population.

From its earliest stages, the Thermonuclear Revolution has caused a mobilization of scientific resources for investigative tasks with military applications. The universities and research centers enlisted in this effort have lost a large measure of autonomy, and their capacity to function as centers of independent thought and free cultural creativity has been diluted. In the early days, scientists were viewed as part wise men and part magicians, and this gave them the illusion that they were finally assuming the reins of power. With the passage of time, however, their influence has been progressively reduced until they now play a merely advisory role to high civilian, military, and business hierarchies, which are not predisposed to abdicate their control. In addition, scientists have been subjected to annoying and oppressive kinds of political surveillance, and simultaneously obliged to face—with tied hands—the ethical problems that derive from their new power to release natural forces able to exterminate all forms of life (Whitaker, 1965; Snow, 1959; Price, 1965).

As a cultural factor, science has thus been transformed from an abstract expression of human efforts to understand experience into the most effective agent ever known for manipulating nature, for reorganizing societies, and for shaping human personalities. Three basic factors are responsible for this change in role. First, the exponential increase in scientific knowledge during the 20th century has been accompanied by a drastic reduction in the interval between the announcement of theoretical discoveries and their practical application, resulting in the fusion of science and technology into a single entity on the operative plane. For example, the experiments of Faraday (1821) preceded the integration of electric motors into the productive system (1886) by 65 years. Later, the lag between the studies of Maxwell and Hertz and the commercialization of radio equipment was reduced to 35 years (1887–1922). In recent decades, progressively shorter intervals have elapsed, as shown by comparing the dates of the theoretical formulation and the technological materialization of radar (1935–1940), the atomic bomb (1938–1945), the transistor (1948–1951), and the solar battery (1953–1955).

Secondly, the professions of scientist and advanced technician, which were viewed as unusual or even eccentric at the beginning of this century, now constitute the normal occupation for growing numbers of people, who today must total close to a million. Their rate of increase has been as rapid as that of factory workers was during the first stage of the Industrial Revolution. As happened in that case, the new contingent will tend in coming decades to absorb the whole working population and ultimately all of humanity, unless the present tendency represents an incidental deviation that is destined for self-correction. Subsequent correction of the curve, however, will not forestall the total transformation of societies that are being exposed to the impact of the new revolution.

A third factor is the fantastic expansion of capital investment in scientific research and technological development. Expenditures of this nature by the United States government quadrupled between 1920 and 1940. For every dollar expended in 1920, $35 were spent in 1950, and $175 in 1960. In absolute numbers, this represents an increase from $80 million in 1920 to about $16 billion in 1963. There is every indication that Russian investments in scientific research and technology are even higher, and that the Chinese are coming ever closer to equaling these magnitudes. An indirect measure of the exponential nature of this increase is provided by the fantastic expansion in the number of scientific publications, which already tend to double in quantity every 15 years. The world output of scientific-technical journals has reached the incredible total of fifty thousand, in which close to a million articles are published annually (Bell, 1964).

The technological revolution now in progress dramatically supports the observation by Marx of the functional relationship between the rate of increase in productivity and the character of social relations surrounding production. In other words, what amount of technological-productive change can modern societies tolerate without a breakdown in their institutional structure? The effects of the new productive processes on labor relations are only beginning to be measurable. Small ruptures and traumas are accumulating, however, that tomorrow will open into fissures extending through the whole society, and which can be breached only by the shaping of new formations. The initial consequences are recognizable in the form of mechanical discongruities between the sources of energy and the machines that consume it, or between machines and raw materials, or even between machines and other machines—which already require periodic replacement of whole sectors of production. Examples include the obsolescence of chemical industrial equipment, or textile machines that are unadaptable to synthetic fibers. More serious disparities exist on the human level. These are manifested in the obsolescence of certain professions (such as firemen on steam locomotives, which have been replaced by diesel or electric engines), leaving their practitioners dislocated and obliged to readjust, an adaptation that they are frequently unsuccessful in making.

Such maladjustments tend to affect limited sectors of the work force at first, then to create masses of displaced labor, and finally to generate multitudes of socially and occupationally marginal people who are condemned to live on pensions from the state. Control of tendencies toward disobedience or rebellion on the part of these displaced masses is a much greater challenge than that faced by the first industrialized societies, which could export human surpluses to colonial areas or consume them in wars. The new social problems cannot be solved so simply, however, because they reflect a severe and growing incompatibility between the social order and the productive technology, and because impulses for social reorganization have already begun to mold societies of a new type whose populations are likely to be more capable of resisting oppression. The tenacity exhibited by the United States Negro in his fight against racial discrimination provides an example of this new capacity among marginal segments in advanced societies.

The principal source of tension is the readjustment required by the conversion of workers from manipulators of tools to operators of machines and finally to supervisors of highly automated productive systems. These systems not only require few workers, but they have no need for either human muscular energy or professional training. On the other hand, they demand ever higher educational qualifications on the part of their supervisors. Thus automation of industry brings about, first of all, a massive reduction in the number of workers. This is followed by a progressive elimination of the "worker aristocracy," composed of highly specialized laborers, and its replacement by a new contingent of more generalized and intellectualized operators, who increasingly resemble the older categories of bureaucrats or the modern type of engineer.

This maze of mechanical and human discordancies, in addition to necessitating readjustments in the factory, the labor force, and institutions of social welfare, also necessitates a complete revision of the educational system. The transformation of scholasticism into a drastic social selector, which excludes the uneducated from the job market, makes it essential that all levels of education be accessible to the entire population. Total revision of the curriculum is required to reflect the extent of integration of science into the general culture. Finally, members of the labor force must have access to a high level of re-education throughout their productive lives.

The impact of these effects on socialist societies, although enormous, is not crucial because it serves mainly to accelerate changes already under way. For capitalistic regimes, however, the impact is a serious challenge because the precedence given to private over public interests leads to inhibition of the kind of socio-economic programming required to bring about the needed reforms. In the face of deepening conflicts, the latter societies tend to react obstinately in an effort to prevent the technological revolution from endangering vested interests and threatening traditional power structures. As a consequence, realization of the potentialities for increased productivity becomes conditional to consolidation of the existing regime, and exhaustive use is made of improved systems of mass communication to mold a submissive and favorable public opinion. Similar attempts to maintain the *status quo* have been made in the past by all privileged classes that have been rendered obsolete. All have ultimately failed, but the course of resistance has frequently led to extreme degradation under despotic and military regimes. This risk is even greater today because technological development has simultaneously brought about a concentration and fusion of economic, political, and military power and permitted a fantastic expansion of the media for informing and molding public opinion. Under these circumstances, a small elite group can not only gain control of the machinery of state and direct national affairs in accord with its interests, but can even elicit strong support from large portions of the population, which can be persuaded to accept the most irrational theses (as exemplified by Hitler's success).

Paradoxically, these Imperialistic Industrial formations are becoming increasingly daring in the technological and economic sector at the same time that they are becoming increasingly conservative on the structural and ideological level. The explanation lies in the climate surrounding the arms race between the United States and the Soviet Union, which has concentrated on maximization of the capacity for retaliation. In both countries, this competition has led to unprecedented emphasis on scientific and technical creativity. In the United States, however, progress has been hampered by the incompatibility between the necessity for directing creativity on the techno-scientific plane (especially in military and space sectors) and at the same time for repressing rational programming on the social and ideological planes.

Spurred by the atomic terror, military and business sectors have begun to promote those aspects of science and technology that are applicable to warfare, the former because it has no choice and the latter because it has been subsidized to do so. Under these conditions, the high levels of the national administrative hierarchy develop into citadels of conservatism where an inordinate confidence in the capacity to utilize scientific-technical progress is combined with a supreme aversion to centralized forms of public administration and control. Since centralization is inevitable, the process of evolutionary transformation becomes extremely discordant; it proceeds lucidly in the scientific-technological sectors and irrationally in the institutional and social ones.

Glaring examples of this conflict emerge with the incorporation of private enterprises into programs of scientific-military research, where instead of manipulating traditional phenomena like productivity, costs, and markets, they must deal with aptitudes and ideas transformed into commodities. One of the lesser problems created by this integration is corruption, which is inherent in situations where public resources are employed to subsidize activities like research, development, or the production of prototypes, when the cost of related plant construction and equipment is included in the contract. So complicated is the situation that an experienced observer has found it impossible to distinguish in the account books of a business those funds expended for normal development from those used in the execution of public contracts (Johnson, 1964). Only extreme dedication to the free-enterprise spirit and an overriding ideological preference for the private management of goods can explain the allocation to private groups of astronomical amounts of public resources under such ambiguous conditions. Some businesses refuse to bid on public projects because of the incompatibility between the usual criteria of efficiency and honesty in producing for the market and the stipulations in government contracts. Others have attempted to keep their private domain free from negotiations with the Treasury by setting up affiliates, the most important of which have been created to exploit the gold mine represented by military contracts.

More severe problems arise from the application of business procedures to the procurement and management of scientists, who are selected by rigorous tests designed to measure their potential capacity for invention. One difficulty stems from the decline in creativity that accompanies increasing age, and this leads some businesses to worry about how to dispose of scientists when they approach the age of 40. Another problem is the decline in scientific return that results from application of additional resources when research is conducted like a business. A further source of conflict is the disparity between the liberal views of scientists and the conservative attitudes prevalent in traditional business sectors of society, which generates an atmosphere laden with tensions in which creative work may become impossible.

All these problems reflect the difficulties of integrating the dynamic new productive technology into a system of private enterprise. This integration is essential, however, for the survival of the capitalistic system. The annual application over the last decade of between two-thirds and three-fifths of the gross national product by the public sectors in the United States would have established a huge system of state enterprises by this time, had it not been for the necessity of channeling technological renovation in such a way as to preserve vested interests. Perpetuation of the private enterprise system has been possible, however, only by its degradation through the adoption of measures such as the allocation of public funds for private use, the abuse of the arms race to stimulate the economy, bureaucratic governmental and military interference in business and, finally, the repression of tensions between labor and management. While such measures alleviate the immediate situation, they do so at the cost of aggravating internal ruptures that will ultimately cause the breakdown of the social structure.

In addition to altering the role of science, the Thermonuclear Revolution seems likely to modify the action of the evolutionary process itself. All previous revolutions have favored those nations that first absorbed the technological innovations and diffused them by the process of historical incorporation, with debilitating effects on the receiving peoples. This revolution, however, tends to initiate new modes of diffusion and generalization of technological progress that will not perpetuate the subordination of backward peoples. Three factors are responsible for this changed situation: (1) competition between socialist and capitalist camps, which has impeded reactionary neo-imperialist efforts; (2) maturation of the ethnos of underdeveloped peoples (clearly evident in the contrast between their impotence a century ago, before imperialistic expansion, and the vigor of resistance today by Algeria against France and Vietnam against the United States); and (3) the Chinese revolution, which set in motion a process of evolutionary acceleration affecting an enormous segment of humanity in the most densely populated, the most destitute, and the most exploited part of the world.

The importance of the Chinese Revolution is implicit in the United Nations demographic prediction that 1800 of the 6000 million human beings alive in the year A.D. 2000 will be Chinese. Another significant factor is the movement toward political, economic, and cultural emancipation underway in underdeveloped countries. Bursting out simultaneously throughout the world, this demand for independence threatens to destroy the neo-colonial basis of the imperialist system and to bring about new international alignments. In the process, underdeveloped peoples assume the role of civilizers of the more advanced ones, paralleling the paradox pointed out by Hegel that history has allocated to the slave the task of fighting for freedom.

Operating on a humanity already integrated into a single interactive system and on peoples determined to utilize their opportunities for autonomous development, the Thermonuclear Revolution should proceed by evolutionary acceleration and progressively integrate the whole world into the same technology and way of life. The advantages attained by the most advanced societies may tempt them to turn inward upon themselves, in order to enjoy the fruits of their progress. Dependence on the world system of interchange, however, will oblige them to interact with less developed peoples. As the latter become increasingly able to defend their own interests, they will impose less exploitative forms of international relations. The extreme disparities in the tempo of evolution that are characteristic today in different parts of the world will thus be greatly reduced. Equalization is favored both by the essential unity of the human species, which makes mankind everywhere equally capable of progress, and by the nature of cultural evolution which, unlike biological evolution, proceeds by symbolic transmission and is therefore rapidly diffusable to all mankind. Realization of this potential, however, requires the creation of world-wide systems of diffusion and education that will make possible the socialization of each new generation in terms of the same content and standards of behavior.

The new evolutionary stage now moving forward along all these roads will once again transform the condition of mankind. This transformation will be more radical than ever before because, for the first time, the modeling action of a technological revolution is directed by a scientifically based international policy. As science moves more completely from the ideological plane to the adaptive one, rational human intervention will increasingly take over the making of history.

Before this is accomplished, however, many obstacles must be overcome. A major one is the shortage of food, clothing, shelter, sanitation, and education that today afflicts most of humanity. This situation is intimately related to the concentration of present-day scientific and technological efforts on destructive activities, and the resultant allocation of an insignificant proportion of resources to the search for improved solutions to the problems created by these critical shortages in goods and services. For example, of the body of scientists and technicians in the United States, 140,000 are employed in aeronautical, space, and electronic military research, but only 1200 are investigating problems of the textile industry, only 4000 are studying the building industry, and only 5000 are involved in metallurgical research (Ginzberg, 1964).

Another problem is the overcoming of the intrinsically spoilative character of interaction between social structures of unequal technological development, which drives underdeveloped peoples to wars of emancipation and bloody revolutions in the effort to acquire minimal autonomy in the pursuit of their destinies. An allied problem is the surmounting of the structural rigidity developed by the imperialistic nations, whose vested interest in the *status quo* leads to internal political domination by minority groups that are dedicated to maintaining the system at any price. The cost of this feat is a heavy burden in military expenditures and in the subsidy of puppet regimes. Under these adverse circumstances, the system is able to continue only because of the political lethargy of the majority, who subsidize it with increasing taxes.

Also relevant to this situation are class differences and racial discrimination, which still impose their dehumanizing effects on the majority of mankind. Both may be eliminated through the evolutionary acceleration generated by the Thermonuclear Revolution itself in the course of shaping the Future Societies. Their elimination will not come about spontaneously, however, because it requires extraordinary efforts of the kind that are possible only with rigorous planning and the fullest international cooperation.

The characteristics of these Future Societies are as little predictable today as the formations contained in the Industrial Revolution were during the first decades of its impact. Nevertheless, some features are already dis-

cernible, and these indicate that the Future Societies will be socialist formations of a new type. They will probably not be stratified into economic
classes, but will be infinitely superior in organization to the undifferentiated
tribal communities that humanity left behind some ten thousand years ago,
and in which personal and egalitarian relationships prevailed. They will
also be a higher type of "socialism" than that exemplified by the Theocratic
Irrigation Empires, which were also based on state ownership of property
and which, in their early stages, were regimes of high social responsibility
and integration, but which ultimately declined into markedly despotic militaristic statism. They will likewise be superior to both evolutionary and revolutionary forms of present-day socialism.

Both Socialistic Revolutionary and Socialistic Evolutionary formations
seem to be converging in this general direction. Existing imperialistic formations will probably follow as their neo-classical context becomes emancipated, and as they themselves throw off privatistic interests and move toward evolutionary socialism. This is also the direction being taken by
modern neo-colonial nations along the alternative paths of modernizing
nationalism or revolutionary socialism, both of which restrain imperialistic
exploitation, reduce internal oligarchical constriction, and permit the maturation of industrialization.

An already evident characteristic of Future Societies is the eradication of
differences between city and country, as a result of the industrialization of
agricultural activities and the expansion of cities over the adjoining landscape. Another characteristic will be the disappearance of the distinction
between physical labor, which will be essentially eliminated, and intellectual labor. The work force will be composed mainly of college graduates
devoted to educational, social service, cultural, and recreational tasks, all of
which will be enormously expanded in number and variety. This higher
level of education will also make the general human cultural heritage accessible to the majority of mankind, and will permit a significant proportion
of the population to make artistic and intellectual contributions.

The alienation of the producer from his product, which was initiated by
the commercialization of craftsmanship and accelerated by industrialization, will be overcome, and each person will once again be able to express
himself in what he does. The love of beauty, which dawned very early in
human societies—where it was expressed in all kinds of objects of greater
perfection and workmanship than were required for utility—and which was

early submerged by the demands of mechanization and specialization, will flourish again. The closed circles now formed by isolated artists and erudite connoisseurs will be broken, and art once more will become a universal activity.

A third characteristic of Future Societies will be their ability to function in a world of almost unlimited possibilities, both in knowledge and in action, and of both constructive and destructive types. The minimal control of these capacities required to prevent their turning against man will bring about the abolition of wars and the creation of a world power structure along supra-national principles, in which human populations will be represented proportionally to their size. It will also involve the development of international agencies for the regulation and dissemination of mass information and for the molding of public opinion.

Once the problems of elimination of shortages and the social regulation of abundance, and of equalization of educational opportunity and generalization of public health facilities have been solved, the primary challenges confronting Future Societies will cease to be their effective use of the prodigious resources of energy, goods, and services. Instead, there will be new problems related to the appropriate use of the power of compulsion over men and the rational application of the socialization process. Future Societies are likely to face their most serious challenges in determining the proper utilization of their nearly absolute powers for the programming of human reproduction, for the intentional organization of social life, for the formation and regulation of the human personality, and for systematic intervention in the values that guide personal behavior. Such tremendous powers inevitably carry with them enormous risks of despotism, but they also offer greater possibilities than ever before for liberating mankind from all forms of fear and oppression.

Tocqueville, who foresaw maturation of the despotic and depersonalizing tendencies perceptible even in 1835, made the following forecast of Future Societies:

> I seek to trace the novel features under which despotism may appear in the world. The first thing that strikes the observation is an innumerable multitude of men, all equal and alike, incessantly endeavoring to procure the petty and paltry pleasures with which they glut their lives. Each of them, living apart, is as a stranger to the fate of all the rest; his children and his private friends constitute to him the

whole of mankind. As for the rest of his fellow citizens, he is close to them, but he does not see them; he touches them, but he does not feel them; he exists only in himself and for himself alone; and if his kindred still remain to him, he may be said at any rate to have lost his country.

Above this race of men stands an immense and tutelary power, which takes upon itself alone to secure their gratifications and to watch over their fate. That power is absolute, minute, regular, provident, and mild. It would be like the authority of a parent if, like that authority, its object was to prepare men for manhood; but it seeks, on the contrary, to keep them in perpetual childhood: it is well content that the people should rejoice, provided they think of nothing but rejoicing. For their happiness such a government willingly labors, but it chooses to be the sole agent and the only arbiter of that happiness; it provides for their security, foresees and supplies their necessities, facilitates their pleasures, manages their principal concerns, directs their industry, regulates the descent of property, and subdivides their inheritances; what remains, but to spare them all the care of thinking and all the trouble of living?*(1960, vol. 2: p. 318)*.

One of the principal challenges facing Future Societies is to overcome the tendencies toward despotism that preoccupied Tocqueville. To be successful, they will have to place maximum emphasis on the cultivation and stimulation of the free development of the human personality, on the encouragement of all forms of creative expression, and on the exploitation of human potentialities for the development of sympathetic and socially responsible behavior.

In 1859, Marx also attempted to anticipate the nature of Future Societies. His view was an optimistic one, which saw organized prosperity not as a condemnation, but rather as a means of liberation of all human potentialities:

In fact, however, when the narrow bourgeois form has been peeled away, what is wealth, if not the universality of needs, capacities, enjoyments, productive powers, etc., of individuals produced in universal exchange? What, if not the full development of human control over the forces of nature—those of his own nature as well as those of so-called "nature"? What, if not the absolute elaboration of his creative

dispositions, without any preconditions other than antecedent historical evolution which makes the totality of his evolution—i.e. the
evolution of all human powers as such, unmeasured by any *previously
established* yardstick—an end in itself? What is this, if not a situation
where man does not reproduce himself in any determined form, but
produces his totality? Where he does not seek to remain something
formed by the past, but is in the absolute movement of becoming?

(1965, pp. 84–85).

Whether the immediate future of the most advanced societies will be
that envisioned by Tocqueville or by Marx will depend on whether the inherent potentialities for despotism or for liberty become accentuated. The
more distant future will certainly resemble that predicted by Marx. It will
be crystallized in the course of a civilizational process that will mature
with the expansion of the Thermonuclear Revolution, and it will no longer
be denotable by an ethnic, racial, or regional adjective. It can be known
only as Universal Civilization.

Summary

Recapitulation of the stages of sociocultural evolution set forth in this essay shows them to begin with the emergence of human societies from a hunting-and-gathering tribal condition as a consequence of the *Agricultural Revolution*, disseminated via two civilizational processes. One produced the first *Undifferentiated Horticultural Villages* about 10,000 years ago and the other created the *Nomadic Pastoral Hordes* somewhat later. Both processes subsequently expanded until they embraced the whole world. In the course of their development, they dynamized the life of peoples everywhere, integrating most of them into the new technologies but relegating others to a backward role, in which some still remain today. Their crucial effect was to crystallize two distinct ways of life, one agricultural and the other pastoral, that continued for millennia to mold human existence.

The Agricultural Revolution was followed by the *Urban Revolution* as a result of the accumulation of technological progress and correlated changes in social structure and ideology. Under the influence of this second technological revolution and of one of its two derivative civilizational processes, some societies were transformed into *Rural Craftsman States* of a *Collectivistic* or *Privatistic* type. These developed *in situ* on a foundation of political and ethnic unity, and bifurcated into urban and rural contingents, both of them stratified into economic classes. The other civilizational process advanced some hordes into *Nomadic Pastoral Chiefdoms*, which were socially less differentiated and culturally less advanced than the Rural Craftsman States, but much more warlike. Conflicts between farmers and herders played a dynamic role in the historic process from this time onward, contributing to the evolutionary acceleration of some peoples, to the loss of autonomy by many others through movements of historical incorporation, and to the creation of multi-ethnic entities with tendencies toward expansionism. Where pastoral peoples were absent because of the lack of animals suitable for riding or traction, as in the Americas, cultural evolution took a slower and less tumultuous form.

With the inception of the *Irrigation Revolution* some 7000 years ago, there appeared the first *Regional Civilizations* in the form of *Theocratic Irrigation Empires*, stimulated by a technology related primarily to irrigation. Application of this technology to other areas and its subsequent perfection led to the eruption of a number of other kinds of technological innovations. Some 3000 years ago, these matured as the *Metallurgical Revolution*, which brought into being the *Mercantile Slavistic Empires*. After successive flowerings and declines, corresponding to successive distinct civilizations, representatives of both these sociocultural formations fell into long periods of feudal regression that were provoked both by exhaustion of their civilizational potential and by attacks from marginal peoples, especially the Nomadic Pastoral Chiefdoms, which had adopted the metallurgical technology and other innovations from their civilized neighbors.

The *Pastoral Revolution,* which took place during the first centuries of our era, provoked the first ruptures with feudalism that did not represent merely restoration of the same type of formation. It emerged with the maturation of Nomadic Pastoral Chiefdoms that had adopted iron technology and messianic religious doctrines, and which then fell upon feudalized areas. Armed with the new technology and an ideology that legitimized and sanctified their zeal, these pastoral groups were able to conquer large sedentary populations and to organize them into *Despotic Salvationist Empires*.

There followed the *Mercantile Revolution,* which was maturing during the 15th century largely as a consequence of advances in oceanic navigation and the perfection of firearms, and which led to a second break with feudalism, this time from within. This Revolution simultaneously exploded over the world from two centers, one on the Iberian peninsula and the other in Russia. Both these centers derived their energy for expansion from reorientation of the resources that had originally been mobilized for reconquest of their own territories, in the former case from the Moslems and in the latter from the Mongol-Tartars. The resulting *Salvationistic Mercantile Empires* were only incipiently capitalistic, and were profoundly imbued with religious motivations and despotic traditions. As peninsular peoples, the Iberians expanded overseas and organized the first world empire based on slavistic colonialism. The Russians, occupying a continental area, launched a mercantile colonization of neighboring populations and integrated large extensions of Eurasia into a single sociopolitical system.

The same technological revolution simultaneously brought a restoration of the European mercantile system and with it the maturation of another sociocultural formation, the *Capitalistic Mercantile Empires.* The stagnation into which feudalized Europe had fallen was destroyed, and a new civilizational process was set in motion that again expanded over the entire world. The Capitalistic Mercantile formation, like the Salvationistic Mercantile Empires, bifurcated into two opposing but complementary segments: One was represented by the metropolitan centers with predominantly capitalistic economies and the other by their objects of exploitation, the *Slavistic, Trading,* or *Immigrant Colonies.*

A new evolutionary leap forward occurred three hundred years later with the *Industrial Revolution,* based on a technology that could exploit inanimate energy. This led some of the most advanced capitalist societies into a new sociocultural formation, the *Imperialistic Industrial Powers,* which was also bifurcated into two complexes: the ruling centers situated in various continents and the *Neo-Colonial Dependencies.* The latter incorporated both former areas of colonial domination and those independent nations that failed to integrate their productive systems into an industrial technology—and which consequently fell into a condition of dependence and reflex modernization via historical incorporation.

During the course of World War I the tensions generated by the maturing Industrial Revolution created another sociocultural formation, the *Socialistic Revolutionary Nations.* Through a process of evolutionary acceleration, these nations expanded over areas that were peripheral to the capitalist system and so raised certain backward countries to the level of modern industrial societies. Later, some Imperialistic Industrial formations, deprived of their colonial contexts and propelled by internal processes of social restructurization, began to change into another formation, that of the *Socialistic Evolutionary Nations.* Finally, certain colonial or neo-colonial peoples succeeded in becoming *Nationalistic Modernizing States* through revolutionary movements of national emancipation from external imperialistic exploitation and against the internal oligarchical structures opposed to development.

The two most recent technological revolutions—the Mercantile and the Industrial—have inaugurated a crucial stage of sociocultural evolution by setting in motion the first world-wide civilizational processes. These placed in interaction all the peoples of the world, arousing some that had been slumbering in a tribal condition, activating others that were still structured as Rural Craftsman or Nomadic Pastoral economies, and subjugating the two Theocratic Irrigation Empires of the Americas, as well as those Witness Peoples representing ancient civilizations immersed in feudalism. All these varied formations have been incorporated into a single productive and mercantile system in a colonial or neo-colonial context. Mankind has thus become unified within a single framework, within which subsequent civilizational processes will exercise their renovating force. This will lead to the crystallization of a *Universal Civilization* that will extend over the whole planet, propelled by the same basic technology, organized on the same structural lines, and motivated by similar values.

Thus the development and diffusion of industrial technology has laid the foundations for a global civilizational process, one that has the capacity to bring to flower the potentialities for progress among peoples everywhere. It will probably mold them into a new sociocultural formation, toward which both Socialistic Revolutionary and Socialistic Evolutionary societies now appear to be heading. The motivating force of this new civilizational process will be the *Thermonuclear Revolution,* which can be expected not only to homogenize the advanced societies, but also to accelerate the progress and eliminate the backward status of other peoples and to integrate them all into *Future Societies.* Certain basic characteristics of the Thermonuclear Revolution as a civilizational process, such as progressive reduction of class differences, integration of science into the adaptive system, and accelerative rather than incorporative compulsion, may give this formation the capacity to modify the evolutionary process itself. If so, this will place mankind for the first time in a position to direct cultural development.

This scheme of sociocultural evolution recognizes eight technological revolutions (Agricultural, Urban, Irrigation, Metallurgical, Pastoral, Mercantile, Industrial, and Thermonuclear), which give rise to twelve civilizational processes responsible for the crystallization of eighteen sociocultural formations, some of which divide into two or more subcomplexes. Feudalism is not conceived here as an evolutionary stage or as a civilizational process that generates a specific sociocultural formation. Rather, it is a cultural regression that results from socio-economic stagnation, and it consequently can appear in any society that has attained the level of urban civilization. This regressive condition can only be temporarily superseded until the inception of a new technological revolution permits such cyclical movements to be surmounted. This is what happened following the Mercantile Revolution when Europe became the center of new civilizational processes that expanded over the entire world. The first breakthrough came in two marginal areas, Iberia and Russia, which were shaped by the Mercantile Revolution into incipiently capitalist formations susceptible to dips into feudalism. Later, maturation of the first Capitalistic Mercantile formations gave to the northern and central European nations, which up until that time had been relatively retarded, several centuries of hegemony over the rest of the world.

The fact that these vital steps in cultural evolution first took place in Europe has colored the civilizational processes by which the technology was disseminated with a unique ideological content. As a consequence, Capitalistic Mercantile and Imperialistic Industrial developments have assumed a Western European and Christian profile, as if these ethnic-cultural and religious attributes were an integral part of the technology of navigation, firearms, or internal combustion engines. These technological accomplishments and the power deriving from them thus became identified as "white man's exploits," and accepted as evidence of an innate European superiority over the rest of the world. In truth, however, they represent natural and necessary steps in human progress, steps which if they had not matured on European soil would have inevitably taken place elsewhere, perhaps in an Islamic, Chinese, or Indian context.

The fact that the Mercantile and Industrial Revolutions did occur in Europe, however, has permitted the Europeanization of a large segment of humanity. This process continued until the 20th century, when there crystallized a polycentric civilization in which the old centers in Europe were converted into secondary nuclei as a consequence of the release of the potentialities for progress among various non-European peoples. Concomitantly, the ideological deception that equated technological precocity with intrinsic racial or religious superiority has been exposed.

Two crucial forces have recently been added to the renovative effects of the Industrial Revolution. The first is the Thermonuclear Revolution, which has wrought a prodigious alteration in the productive system, has transformed science into an effective agent of change, and has destroyed the economic foundation for social inequality. The second is the tremendous acceleration of progress, which has aggravated social tensions and will force the destruction of existing sociocultural formations, permitting the underdeveloped nations to catch up with the developed ones. The convergent action of these two forces will homogenize and integrate all the peoples of the world into a single Universal Civilization, which cannot be identified with any individual race or cultural tradition. It will also place within the reach of mankind for the first time the capacity to direct the evolutionary process itself.

Viewed as a whole, this scheme of sociocultural evolution is multilinear, since it allows for varying forms of transition from a tribal to an agro-pastoral condition, and from the latter to regional civilization and, finally, to modern society (Frontispiece). It also sees each technological revolution as operating through civilizational processes, which expand by successive waves, thus increasing the areas of diffusion of new technologies and continuing to modify populations even after the inception of later revolutions. The latter, in turn, influence peoples who may or may not have been reached by previous revolutions, reshaping them and affecting in different manners their ways of life and their prospects for development, depending on whether they act as externally directed movements of historical incorporation or through internal evolutionary acceleration.

The combination of these technological revolutions, civilizational processes, and various sociocultural formations makes it possible to speak of a global civilizational process that is divided into successive stages. Although these stages are represented by peoples separated from each other in time and space, they reflect the reorganization of human life over increasingly larger areas, and integration into political and ethnic entities of growing size, culminating with unification of all humanity into a single interactive context (Figure 2). Through this process the human species, originally small in size and divided into innumerable ethnic groups, has been multiplied demographically and reduced in cultural and linguistic diversity. Over the millenia, this trend seems likely to culminate in the creation of a single (or very few) racial, cultural, and linguistic entity.

Finally, the evolutionary scheme proposed here brings out the fact that the successive technological revolutions have been proceeding at an increasingly rapid rate, and that simultaneously their power of compulsion and breadth of action have progressively enlarged. Humanity required about a million years to build the foundations for the Agricultural Revolution, which began in a few groups about 10,000 years ago. This was followed, first by the Urban Revolution, which matured originally some 7000 years ago, and then by the Irrigation Revolution, which was expressed some 2500 years later with the appearance of the first Regional Civilizations. The Metallurgical Revolution, initiated 1500 years later, was succeeded after only about 1200 years by the Pastoral Revolution. The lapse between the latter and the Mercantile Revolution was reduced to 700 years, while the next interval, which brought the Industrial Revolution, was shortened to 300 years. Finally, the Thermonuclear Revolution, flowering at the present time, has appeared after an even briefer interval.

As a consequence of this accelerating rate of change, two successive generations today differ more in experience and world view than did a hundred successive generations in the past. The cumulative character of technological progress and its increasing momentum make it probable that the next few decades of this century will bring even more rapid and radical transformations. By traveling this path, man, who won the battle for survival in competition with other species and who developed a culture that permitted the subjugation of nature for human benefit, has terminated by finding himself submerged in a cultural milieu much more oppressive than his physical environment, and confronted with the challenge of bending culture to his needs. If he is successful, culture, the creator, and man, the created, will become blended; man will be humanized by culture, and culture will be molded by the human conscience. The result will permit man to influence his own biological, social, cultural, and psychological reproduction, and to shape himself by his own plan.

There is nothing to suggest that there are limits to man's flexibility for adjusting to the most diverse conditions. The question can be raised, however, whether the increasingly oppressive conditioning to cultural environments, and the challenge of consciously intervening in cultural development may not endanger human survival. The menaces that hang over mankind, both in the form of super-destructive wars that threaten biological degradation of the species and in the form of collapse into despondency and disillusionment as a consequence of deterioration in moral values, raise

WORLD CIVILIZATIONS

Salvationistic Mercantile Empires

Spain (1500)
Portugal (1500)
Russia (1500)

Slavistic Colonies

Spanish America (1500)
Brazil (1550)
British Antilles (1650)

Capitalistic Mercantile Empires

Holland (1600)
England (1650)
France (1700)

Trading Colonies

Indonesia (1600–1945)
Angola (since 1648)
India (1876–1945)

Immigrant Colonies

North America (1650)
Australia (1850)

Imperialistic Industrial Powers

England (1750)
France (1800)
United States (1840)
Japan (1900)

Neo-Colonial Dependencies

Brazil
Venezuela
India

Socialistic Revolutionary Nations

USSR (1917)
Eastern Europe (1945)
China (1949)
North Korea (1948)
North Vietnam (1954)
Cuba (1959)

Socialistic Evolutionary Nations

Sweden (1945)
Denmark (1950)
England (1965)

Nationalistic Modernizing States

Mexico (1940)
Egypt (1953)
Algeria (1962)

REGIONAL CIVILIZATIONS

Theocratic Irrigation Empires

Akkad (2350 B.C.)
Egypt I (2070 B.C.)
Babylonia (1800 B.C.)
Maurya (327 B.C.)
Chin and Han (220 B.C.)
Tang (618)
Gupta (320)
Chimu (1000)
Aztec (1400)
Inca (1400)

Mercantile Slavistic Empires

Assyria (1200 B.C.)
Achaemenia (600 B.C.)
Carthage (600 B.C.)
Greece (450 B.C.)
Rome (27 B.C.)

Despotic Salvationist Empires

Sassanean (224)
Islamic (651)
Byzantine (1025)
Ottoman (1460)
Timurid (1530)

ARCHAIC SOCIETIES

Undifferentiated Horticultural Villages

Jarmo (5000 B.C.)
Fayum (4500 B.C.)
Mamom (500 B.C.)
Marajoara (1000)
Tupinamba (1500)
Kwakiutl
Zuni
Ifugao
Dobu
Tikopia

Nomadic Pastoral Hordes

Mbaya
Comanche
Chukchi
Nuer
Sakalave

Rural Craftsman States

Uruk, Ur, Kish
(4000–3000 B.C.)
Eridu, Memphis, Thebes
(1400–2500 B.C.)
Mohenjo-daro, Harappa
(2800 B.C.)
Hsia, Yang-Shao (2000 B.C.)
Tyre, Sidon, Byblos
(2000–1000 B.C.)
Mycenaea (1700 B.C.)
Urartu (1000 B.C.)
Marib (700 B.C.)
Athens (550 B.C.)
Khmer (500 B.C.)
Rome (350 B.C.)
Mochica (200 B.C.)
Uxmal (300)
Ghana (800)
Chibcha (1000)
Mali (1200)

Nomadic Pastoral Chiefdoms

Hyksos (1750 B.C.)
Hittites (1600 B.C.)
Kassites (1600 B.C.)
Aryans (1300 B.C.)
Sea Peoples (1200 B.C.)
Scythians (500 B.C.)
Huns, (   )
Sakas (120 B.C.)
Teutons (400)
Vandals (400)
Visigoths (400)
Hungarians (600)
Arabs (600)
Turks (600)
Mongols (1200)
Manchus (1500)

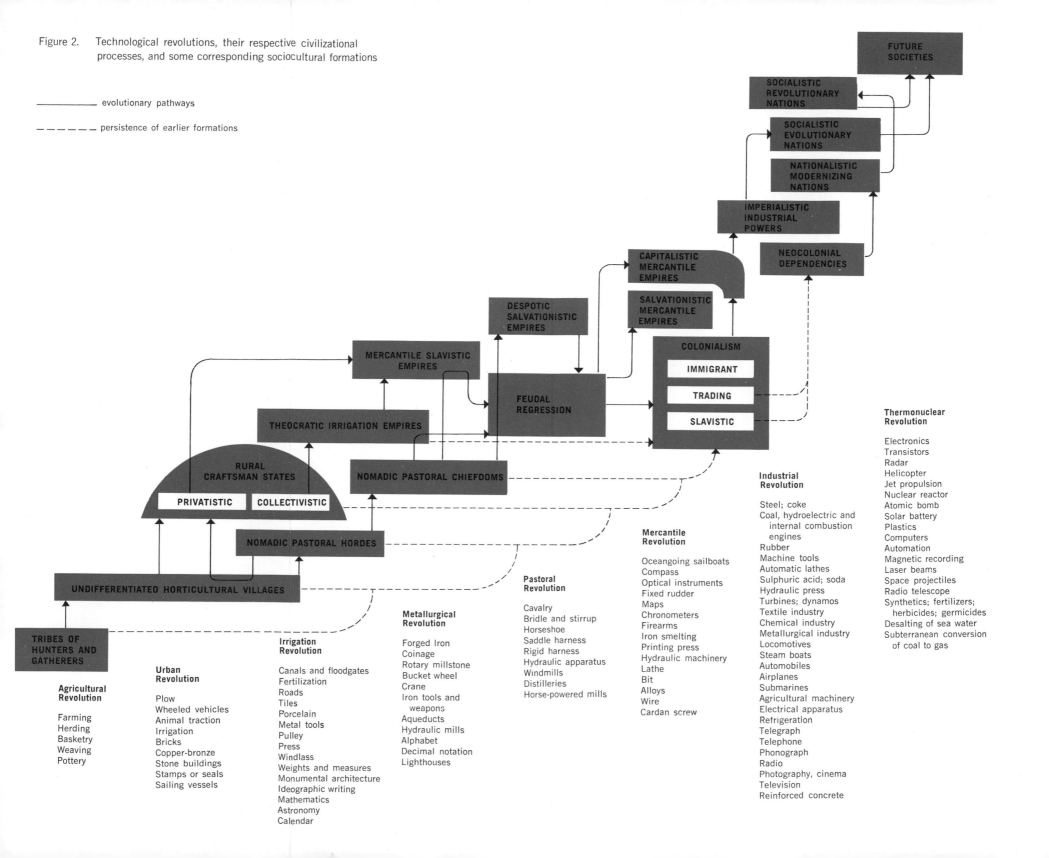

Figure 2.   Technological revolutions, their respective civilizational
             processes, and some corresponding sociocultural formations

—————— evolutionary pathways

- - - - - persistence of earlier formations

FUTURE SOCIETIES

SOCIALISTIC REVOLUTIONARY NATIONS

SOCIALISTIC EVOLUTIONARY NATIONS

NATIONALISTIC MODERNIZING NATIONS

IMPERIALISTIC INDUSTRIAL POWERS

NEOCOLONIAL DEPENDENCIES

CAPITALISTIC MERCANTILE EMPIRES

SALVATIONISTIC MERCANTILE EMPIRES

DESPOTIC SALVATIONISTIC EMPIRES

MERCANTILE SLAVISTIC EMPIRES

COLONIALISM

IMMIGRANT

TRADING

SLAVISTIC

FEUDAL REGRESSION

THEOCRATIC IRRIGATION EMPIRES

RURAL CRAFTSMAN STATES

PRIVATISTIC   COLLECTIVISTIC

NOMADIC PASTORAL CHIEFDOMS

NOMADIC PASTORAL HORDES

UNDIFFERENTIATED HORTICULTURAL VILLAGES

TRIBES OF HUNTERS AND GATHERERS

Agricultural Revolution

Farming
Herding
Basketry
Weaving
Pottery

Urban Revolution

Plow
Wheeled vehicles
Animal traction
Irrigation
Bricks
Copper-bronze
Stone buildings
Stamps or seals
Sailing vessels

Irrigation Revolution

Canals and floodgates
Fertilization
Roads
Tiles
Porcelain
Metal tools
Pulley
Press
Windlass
Weights and measures
Monumental architecture
Ideographic writing
Mathematics
Astronomy
Calendar

Metallurgical Revolution

Forged Iron
Coinage
Rotary millstone
Bucket wheel
Crane
Iron tools and
   weapons
Aqueducts
Hydraulic mills
Alphabet
Decimal notation
Lighthouses

Pastoral Revolution

Cavalry
Bridle and stirrup
Horseshoe
Saddle harness
Rigid harness
Hydraulic apparatus
Windmills
Distilleries
Horse-powered mills

Mercantile Revolution

Oceangoing sailboats
Compass
Optical instruments
Fixed rudder
Maps
Chronometers
Firearms
Iron smelting
Printing press
Hydraulic machinery
Lathe
Bit
Alloys
Wire
Cardan screw

Industrial Revolution

Steel; coke
Coal, hydroelectric and
   internal combustion
   engines
Rubber
Machine tools
Automatic lathes
Sulphuric acid; soda
Hydraulic press
Turbines; dynamos
Textile industry
Chemical industry
Metallurgical industry
Locomotives
Steam boats
Automobiles
Airplanes
Submarines
Agricultural machinery
Electrical apparatus
Refrigeration
Telegraph
Telephone
Phonograph
Radio
Photography, cinema
Television
Reinforced concrete

Thermonuclear Revolution

Electronics
Transistors
Radar
Helicopter
Jet propulsion
Nuclear reactor
Atomic bomb
Solar battery
Plastics
Computers
Automation
Magnetic recording
Laser beams
Space projectiles
Radio telescope
Synthetics; fertilizers;
   herbicides; germicides
Desalting of sea water
Subterranean conversion
   of coal to gas

the possibility that we may be reaching our limits; that we may be taking fatal risks unless rational forms of control for social, economic, and political life are developed. This necessity for a rationalization of social life, for an intentional construction of culture, and for intervention into the world of values that motivate behavior, points to socialism as the form most likely to provide the impersonal systems of control that are indispensible to the creation of freer and more responsible men in an era of abundance. If the challenge is met, the "production" of human beings will at last constitute the be-all and end-all of the civilizational process.

Bibliography

INTRODUCTORY OBSERVATIONS

A theoretical formulation like the one in this volume is inevitably the product of years of thought and experience. Conversations, events, classroom teaching, reading, research, and many other conscious and unconscious influences contribute to the final result. As a consequence, it is impossible to identify and acknowledge with anything approaching completeness the origin of many ideas incorporated in the text. On the other hand, identification of the sources employed by the author assumes special importance in studies of a primarily bibliographic nature. This is even more crucial in the case of a broad and controversial theme like sociocultural evolution, which is the subject of an extensive bibliography that contains theoretical essays and descriptive works of very unequal merit.

In order to improve readability, the specific sources relevant to a particular point of data or theory have rarely been cited in the text. In compensation, however, a detailed review is provided here of those works that proved most useful in the analysis of each of the principal themes. This, I hope, will provide specialists with the information necessary to evaluate the representativeness of the bibliographic material at my disposal, and will also offer the interested reader an opportunity to consult additional sources, should he wish to explore more fully any special aspect of the analysis.

Previous Theoretical Studies and Evolutionary Schemes The primary sources for the present study are previous attempts to recognize the basic principles of sociocultural evolution and to establish the general sequences by which it took place. They can be classified into three groups: the classics of anthropology, Marxist works, and modern anthropological studies.

Outstanding in the first category is the classic work of Lewis H. Morgan, *Ancient Society, or Researches in the Lines of Human Progress from Savagery through Barbarism to Civilization,* published in 1877, which provided the first general scheme of cultural evolution. Other significant contributions were made by Auguste Comte (1840), Edward B. Tylor (1871, 1881), and Herbert Spencer (1895–1897), each of whom systematized and disseminated the notion of social evolution. Of them all, only Morgan remains of more than historical interest today. General evaluations of these works are provided by Barnes and Becker (1938) and Frantsov (1966); more detailed appraisals can be found in White (1945a, 1945b, 1948, 1960), Stern (1931, 1946, 1948), and Opler (1964).

Of the Marxist contributions, the most significant are the works of Karl Marx himself, especially the *Pre-Capitalist Economic Formations* (1965), *A Contribution to the Critique of Political Economy* (1904), and *Capital* (1967). The classic work by Friedrick Engels, *The Origin of the Family* (1942), also falls into this category, as well as his studies on the role of work in the humanizing process (1949, 1964). Also relevant are the explanations of Marxist thinking by Kautzky (1925) and Plekhanov (1940, 1947).

Although the commentaries of Marx on pre-capitalist formations were written between 1857–1859, they were not published until 1939, and only began to be discussed in the 1950's. Their deviation from the evolutionary scheme of Engels and their considerable interpretative value thus have only recently become evident. Appraisals of this contribution can be found in Hobsbawm (1965), Godelier (1964), Chesneaux (1964), and del Barco (1965).

Engels' classic work on *The Origin of the Family* (1942; cf. Stern, 1948) gave rise to an ample literature. Outstanding for his completeness and systematic approach is Viatkin (Ed., n.d.); other significant contributions are those of Kuusinen and others (1963), Makarov (Ed., 1965), and Chesnokov (1966). More original works which represent the same orientation but focus on particular aspects of evolution, include Dobb (1964), Lange (1963, 1966), Sweezy (1942), Baran (1957), Baran and Sweezy (1966), and Sweezy and others (1967).

Among modern anthropological studies that have revived evolutionist theory, those of Childe (1934, 1936, 1944a, 1946, 1951), White (1949, 1959), and Steward (1955) are outstanding. Following the orientation of these scholars, several very interesting efforts have recently appeared, among them Meggers (1960), Service (1962), and the joint contribution edited by Sahlins and Service (1960). Other works of great interest include Palerm (1955), Palerm and Wolf (1961), and Wolf (1959)—which deal particularly with civilizations based on irrigation—and Adams (1966), who has presented a comparative analysis of the evolution of civilization in Mesopotamia and Mexico. Collections of evolutionary studies have been edited by Meggers (1959), Tax (1960), and Barringer and others (1965).

Anti-evolutionist Studies Two anthropological schools of thought, although opposed to (or formulated as alternatives to) evolutionist theory, are nevertheless relevant. Particularly important are the diffusionist or "Kulturkreis" works by Schmidt and Koppers (1924), Graebner (1924), Montandon (1934), Imbelloni (1953), and Laviosa Zambotti (1958, 1959). Several attempts by anthropologists to outline panoramas of the development of civilization, such as those of Kroeber (1944, 1962) and Linton (1955), should also be consulted.

Comparative Analysis of Special Themes Here, the classic works of Durkheim (1964, 1965), Sombart (1964), M. Weber (1947, 1948, 1954), Sorokin (1937–1941, 1950), Mumford (1938, 1961, 1963), Mannheim (1936), and Veblen (1965) have been especially useful. In the same class are the theoretical examinations of social causality by Ogburn (1926) and MacIver (1942), the analysis of rural-urban contrasts by Redfield (1953, 1956), and the polemic monograph on *Oriental Despotism* by Wittfogel (1957); see also the review by Naquet (1964), the studies on the role of women by Beauvoir (1953), and the history of science by J. D. Bernal (1954).

Theories of History Particularly relevant for the study of cultural evolution are several classical and modern works on historical theory, such as that by Spengler (1962), A. Weber (1935), Schrecker (1948), Jaspers (1953), and especially Toynbee (1948–1961). On the latter, comments by Kroeber (1952) and Bentancourt Dias (1961) should also be consulted.

Among the interpretative essays on the philosophy of history, we have profited from the classic works by Condorcet (1955), Hegel (1881), Gumplowicz (1883), Kropotkin (1955), and Novikov (1902), as well as the reconstructions of the cultural profiles of certain civilizations by Burckhardt (1929), Tocqueville (1960), Huizinga (1924), and Berdaieff (1962).

Historical Monographs and Treatises   Sources of particular importance are the historical treatises of Crouzet (1957), J. Pirenne (1962), R. E. Turner (1941), and Hawkes (1963).

We have also profitably consulted a number of archeological, prehistoric, and historical monographs relevant to sociocultural evolution. Outstanding are those by Childe (1934) and Braidwood (1952) on the Middle East, Drioton and Vandier (1952) on Egypt, Pallottino (1955) on the Etruscans, Glotz (1965) on Greece, Rostovtsev (1926) on Rome, Massé (Ed., 1952) on Iran, Gardet (1954) on Islam, Vasiliev (1952) on Byzantium, Wheeler (1953, 1959) and Piggott (1950) on India, Lattimore (1940) and Grousset (1939) on the Tartar-Mongol expansion, Zaburov (1960) and Grousset (1944) on the Crusades, Osgood (1951) on Korea, Maspero (1929–1930) on Indochina, Suret-Canale (1958) on Africa, and Bosch-Gimpera (1960) on the Indo-Europeans.

Americanist Studies   The principal sources on aboriginal cultures of South America are those provided in the various volumes of the *Handbook of South American Indians*, edited by Steward (1946–1950). For the high civilizations, we have also consulted Morley (1946) on the Maya; Vaillant (1941), Caso (1958), and Soustelle (1961) on the Aztec; Armillas (1952), Wolf (1959), and I. Bernal (1953) on Mesoamerica; Bennett (1946), Bennett and Bird (1949), and Steward and Faron (1959) on the Incas. Evolutionarily oriented general sources include the volume edited by Meggers and Evans (1963) on Latin American prehistory and a synthesis by Meggers (ms.) of New World cultural development.

Cultural Dynamics   We consulted with little profit a number of theoretical studies related to culture change and the process of acculturation, such as Redfield, Linton, and Herskovits (1936), Beals (1953), Barnett and others (1954), Aguirre Beltrán (1957), Malinowski (1944, 1945),

Hunter (1956), and Mead (1966). Somewhat more useful are the works of Foster (1960, 1962) and Barnett (1963), and the studies of Balandier (1955; Ed., 1956; Ed., 1958) on colonialism.

Although not dealing directly with cultural dynamics, the following theoretical essays were of great interest: Sapir (1924), Levi-Strauss (1949, 1953), Murdock (1947, 1949), Radcliffe-Brown (1931), Kluckhohn (1953), as well as recent articles by Parsons (1964) and Eisenstadt (1964), who have resumed the evolutionist perspective in the field of sociology.

Evolution and Unequal Development   Results of all attempts to draw upon evolutionary theory for an understanding of the causes of unequal development in modern societies and the means of emerging from a backward condition are as yet unreliable. The best contributions to this subject are by Lenin (1947, 1951, 1956), Trotzky (1967), Baran (1957), Baran and Sweezy (1966), and Frank (1967a). I have provided a copious annotated bibliography on this theme elsewhere (*As Américas e a Civilização*, ms.), and it is only necessary to point out here representative "doctrinaire" studies of reflexive modernization, such as the works of Rostow (1960, 1964), Lerner (1958), Gerschenkron (1962), Silvert (Ed., 1963), Hoselitz (1960), Hagen (1962), Eisenstadt (1963a), and Kuznets (1946, 1964).

Socio-economic studies that explain the causes of unequal development include Myrdal (1957, 1961), Zimmerman (1965), Clairmonte (1960), Moussa (1959), Lacoste (1959), Lebret (1959), Pinto (1967), Furtado (1966), Horowitz (1966), and Schemeliov (1965).

In a collection of anthropological essays related to this theme, edited by Barringer and others (1965), those on the theory of evolution by Campbell and Opler, and on its application by Spengler, Feldman, and Cottrell are outstanding.

Analysis of Ecological, Technological, and Economic Factors   Included in this category are basic works that analyze the role of ecological, technological, and economic factors in sociocultural change, as well as demographic studies.

Especially useful for assessment of the role of ecological factors are

Huntington (1927), Forde (1949), Meggers (Ed., 1956), Gourou (1953), Bates (1952), Castro (1952), and Steward (1950, 1955, Ch. 2).

The principal works consulted on the history of technology and its role in sociocultural evolution are: Singer and others (Eds., 1954–1958), Dumas (Ed., 1963), Marx (1967), Childe (1944a, 1951, 1954, 1956), Leroi-Gourhan (1943, 1945, 1963), Lilley (1948), Cottrell (1955), Zimmermann (1951), Allen (Ed., 1957), Briggs and others (1963), Cipolla (1962), Sayce (1965), and Fleming and Brocklehurst (1925).

Relevant studies dealing with economy include Herskovits (1952)—in spite of his anti-evolutionist attitude—the classic work of Thurnwald (1932), the study of economic anthropology by Berliner (1962), and the recent analyses of hunters and peasants by Sahlins (1968) and Wolf (1966), which are based on an evolutionary perspective. Also highly useful were the comparative articles on aspects of aboriginal cultures published in volume 5 of the *Handbook of South American Indians* (Steward, Ed., 1949) by Bennett, Metraux, O'Neale, Root, Cooper, Kirchhoff, Lowie, Kroeber, Ackerknecht, and Steward, as well as the studies on cultural diffusion by Nordenskiold (1930, 1931) and Schmidt (1926).

On demography, migrations, depopulation, and population increase, I have consulted Childe (1946, 1956), Sauvy (1952–1954, 1961), Landry (1949), Davis (Ed., 1945), Sireau (1966), Cèpéde and others (1964), and Cipolla (1962).

Agriculture and Cultivated Plants   Agriculture and cultivated plants are dealt with by Vavilov (1926), Sauer (1952), Dumont (1957), and Heiser (1965); the work of Curwen and Hatt (1953) on agricultural technology is also relevant. Of special interest are the typology of agricultural communities proposed by Wolf (1966), and the study of the most primitive kinds of horticulture by Conklin (1961).

Ethnos, State, and Nationality   The discussion of ethnos is based on works by Weltfish (1960), Naroll (1964), Znaniecki (1944), Kohn (1945), and Gennep (1922). Also noteworthy is a recent study of tribal ethnos by Sahlins (1968).

In the analysis of nationality and the State, we have drawn upon the classic Marxist scholars—Engels (1942), Lenin (1951), and Stalin

(1940a)—as well as on anthropologists like Radcliffe-Brown (1940), White (1959), Eisenstadt (1963b), Hoebel (1954), Fried (1960, 1967), Service (1962), Southall (1965), and Gluckman and Eggan (1965).

Slavery   On the subject of slavery, we have used works by Viatkin (Ed., n.d.), Kuusinen and others (1963), and Makarov (Ed., 1965). Also highly useful were the observations of Marx (1965) on "ancient classic" formations, of Rostovtsev (1926) on the Roman Empire, and the collection of essays published by Guenther, Schrot, and others (1960), especially those by Kuo on China, and Uchenko, Kovaliev, and Schtaerman on Greece and Rome. Basic sources on slavery in the Americas are Williams (1944), Tannenbaum (1947), and Bagú (1949, 1952).

Feudalism   Here again, the basic references are the books by Marx (1904, 1965, 1967), as well as Engels (1942), Dobb (1964), and Sweezy and others (1967), although I disagree with their concept of feudalism as a progressive evolutionary stage. Also useful are Wittfogel (1957) and Steward (1955, Ch. 11), whose analyses of "cyclical conquests" have been adapted in this volume to demonstrate the regressive nature of feudalism. I have also referred to more general works by Bloch (1961), H. Pirenne (1937), Coulborn (Ed., 1956), Berdaieff (1962), Piettre (1955), and Romero (1967). On this theme, see also Bagú (1949, 1952), Mariátegui (1955), García (1948), Stavenhagen (1965), and Frank (1967a, 1967b).

Urbanization: Cities and Metropolises   On the origin and development of urban life and related problems, such as the role of erudite culture, use has been made of Wirth (1938), Eisenstadt (1963b), Mumford (1938, 1961), Davis (1955), Hoselitz (1953), Redfield and Singer (1954), Dorselaer and Gregory (1962), Hardoy (1964), Sjoberg (1966), Quintero (1964), and Adams (1966).

Stages of Sociocultural Evolution   The most important works I have consulted for the study of technological revolutions and construction of theoretical models of sociocultural formations can be broken down into categories, as follows:

On the so-called "human revolution": Washburn and Howell (1960), Hockett and Ascher (1964), Montagu (1965), Okladnikov (1962), Huxley (1955), and Simpson (1951).

On pre-agricultural formations: Steward (1955, Ch. 7–8), Owen (1965), and Sahlins (1968). I have also drawn upon personal experiences among indigenous groups like the Guajá and Xokléng of Brazil.

For the Agricultural Revolution and Undifferentiated Horticultural Villages, Childe (1934, 1936, 1944a, 1946, 1951), White (1959), and Steward (1955, Ch. 11), are particularly relevant. Also significant is my familiarity with the ethnological bibliography for South America (see Steward, Ed., 1946–1950; Baldus, 1954; Pericot García, 1962; and Armillas, 1963), and my fieldwork, especially among the Urubú-Kaapor Indians and tribes of the Xingú region.

On the pastoral societies I have been able to refer only to texts like Dittmer (1953), historical monographs by Lattimore (1940) and Grousset (1944), and to encyclopedia articles. Here also, however, I have done personal fieldwork with indigenous South American groups that have adopted the horse (Mbaya-Guaikuru), while references dealing with North America have furthered my comprehension of the phenomenon.

On the Urban Revolution and Rural Craftsman States, my basic sources were Childe (1936, 1944b, 1946, 1951), White (1949, 1959), Steward (1955, Ch. 11), and Steward and Faron (1959). I have also utilized Kroeber's (1946) account of the Chibcha, that of Suret-Canale (1958) on the African kingdoms, and those of Hirshman (1945) and Mahan (1890) on the maritime kingdoms.

On the Irrigation Revolution and the Theocratic Irrigation Empires, see Childe (1936, 1946, 1951), Steward (1955, Ch. 11; and Ed. 1955), White (1959), Wittfogel (1955, 1957), and Cunow (1933). Among the pioneering works on the role of irrigation and the nature of societies based thereon, I have considered the observations of Marx on the "mode of Asiatic production" and his writings on India included in the Spanish edition of *Pre-Capitalist Economic Formations*, and also consulted Metchnikov (1889) and Baudin (1961). Among outstanding modern examinations of this theme are those by Armillas (1952), Wolf (1959), Palerm (1955), and Adams (1966). Also highly useful are Braidwood (1952) on the Middle East, Wheeler (1953, 1959) on India, and Creel (1937) on China.

On the Metallurgical Revolution and Mercantile Slavistic Empires,

Childe (1936, 1946, 1951), White (1959), and Marx (1965) have been particularly useful, as well as works by Ferguson (1913) and Rostovtsev (1926) on Rome, Toynbee (1959) and Glotz (1965) on Greek civilization, Pallottino (1955) on the Etruscans, and Vasiliev (1952) on Byzantium.

On the Pastoral Revolution and the Despotic Salvationist Empires, I have especially consulted Levy (1957), Massé (1952), Wittfogel (1957), Toynbee (1948–1961, vol. 2), and Linton (1955).

On the Mercantile Revolution, the Salvationistic Mercantile Empires and the modern forms of Slavistic, Trading, and Immigrant Colonies, Mauro (1964) and M. Weber (1948, 1954) were particularly helpful. On Russian expansion, I have consulted Solovev (1948), Grekov (1947), Nol'de (1952–1953), and Briúsov and others (n.d.).

On Iberian expansion: Sánchez-Albornoz (1946, 1956), Altamira y Crevea (1968), Vicens Vives (1957–1959), Oliveira Martins (1930), Cortesão (1947), and Sergio (1929). Other relevant works are those by Parry (1949) on European expansion, Klein (1964) on the "mesta," and Lea (1908) and Lewin (1962) on the Inquisition. With reference to Spanish-American colonial institutions, I have made use of Bagú (1949, 1952), Ots Capdequi (1946), and Haring (1947).

On Capitalistic Mercantile Empires, the primary sources are Marx (1904, 1967), Viatkin (Ed., n.d.), Cunningham (1911), M. Weber (1954), Sombart (1964), Dobb (1925, 1964), Sweezy and others (1967), Renouvin (1949, Introduction), See (1928), and Mauro (1964).

On the Industrial Revolution, I have consulted Marx (1904, 1967), Schumpeter (1951, 1956), Sternberg (1959), Aron (1967), Pasdermadjian (1960), Clark (1957), Fourastié (1949, 1960), Dahrendorf (1959), Sireau (1966), Cipolla (1962), Rumiantsev (Ed., 1963), Perroux (1961), and Strachey (1956).

On Imperialistic Industrial Powers, see Hobson (1965), Lenin (1947, 1951, 1956), Luxemburg (1951), Schumpeter (1951), Sweezy (1963), Baran (1957), Frank (1967a), Horowitz (1966), and Strachey (1960).

On Neo-Colonialism, Arnault (1958), Balandier (Ed., 1956), Nkrumah (1965), Jalée (1968), Fanon (1965), and Worsley (1964) are primary references. Here, also, my direct familiarity with development problems in Latin America has been extremely useful.

On Neo-Capitalism, I have consulted Berle and Means (1937), Galbraith (1958), and Mendès-France and Ardant (1955). Critical comments have been provided by Strachey (1956), Sweezy (1963), and Baran (1957).

On Socialistic Expansion and Socialistic Revolutionary, Socialistic Evolutionary, and Nationalistic Modernizing Nations, see Lenin (1947, 1951), Trotzky (1965, 1967), Kuusinen and others (1963), Viatkin (Ed., n.d.), Soboliev and others (n.d.), Ponomarev and others (1962), Afanasiev (n.d.), Webb and Webb (1936), Lange (1963, 1966), Dobb (1948), Hodgman and Bergson (Eds., 1954), Mannheim (1944, 1950), Perroux (1958), Sauvy (1952–1954, 1961), Karol (1967), Schemeliov (1965), and Horowitz (1966).

On the Thermonuclear Revolution and Future Societies, I have consulted Wiener (1948, 1950), Oppenheimer (1954), Bell (1960, 1964), Snow (1959), J. D. Bernal (1958), Carr (1951), Laski (1943), Djilas (1957), Fromm (1955), Henry (1963), Myrdal (1961), Ginzberg (Ed., 1964), Arzumanian (1965), Lerner and Lasswell (Eds., 1965), Mills (1956), Toynbee (1948–1961), Halperin (1965, 1967), Kahn (1962), and Holton (Ed., 1965).

REFERENCES

ADAMS, ROBERT McC.

1955 See Steward, Julian H. (Ed.).
1966 *The Evolution of Urban Society: Early Mesopotamia and Prehistoric Mexico.* Chicago (Aldine).

AFANASIEV, V.

n.d. *El Comunismo Científico.* Moscow (Ediciones en Lenguas Extrangeras).

AGUIRRE BELTRÁN, GONZALO

1957 *El Proceso de Aculturación.* México (Universidad Nacional Autónoma).

ALLEN, FRANCIS R. (Ed.).

1957 *Technology and Social Change.* New York (Appleton-Century-Crofts).

ALTAMIRA Y CREVEA, RAFAEL

1968 *A History of Spanish Civilization.* New York (Biblo and Tannen).

ARMILLAS, PEDRO

1952 See Tax, Sol (Ed.).
1963 *Programa de Historia América: Período Indígena.* Mexico (Instituto Panamericano de Geografía e Historia).

ARNAULT, JACQUES

1958 *Procès du Colonialisme.* Paris (Éditions Sociales).

ARON, RAYMOND

1964 *La Lutte des Classes.* Paris (Gallimard).
1967 *18 Lectures on Industrial Society.* London (Weidenfeld and Nicolson).

ARZUMANIAN, A.

1965 *Ideología, Revolución y Mundo Actual.* Buenos Aires (Editorial Arandú).

ASHTON, THOMAS SOUTHCLIFFE

1948 *The Industrial Revolution, 1760–1830.* New York (Oxford Univ. Press).

BAGÚ, SERGIO

1949 *Economía de la Sociedad Colonial.* Buenos Aires (El Ateneo).
1952 *Estructura Social de la Colonia.* Buenos Aires (El Ateneo).

BAKER, WILLIAM O.

1964 See Ginzberg, Eli (Ed.).

BALANDIER, GEORGES

1955 *Sociologie Actuelle de l'Afrique Noire.* Paris (Presses Universitaires de France).

BALANDIER, GEORGES (Ed.).

1956 *Le "Tiers Monde," Sous-développement et Développement.* Paris (Presses Universitaires de France).

1958   *Social, Economic and Technological change: A Theoretical Approach.* Paris (International Social Science Council).

BALDUS, HERBERT

1954   *Bibliografía Crítica de Etnologia Brasileira.* São Paulo.

BARAN, PAUL A.

1957   *The Political Economy of Growth.* New York (Monthly Review Press).

BARAN, PAUL A., and SWEEZY, PAUL M.

1966   *Monopoly Capital: An Essay on the American Economic and Social Order.* New York (Monthly Review Press).

BARNES, HARRY ELMER, and BECKER, HOWARD

1938   *Social Thought from Lore to Science.* Boston, New York (D. C. Heath and Co.).

BARNETT, H. G.

1963   *Innovation: The Basis of Cultural Change.* New York (McGraw Hill).

BARNETT, H. G., and others

1954   "Acculturation: An Exploratory Formulation." *American Anthropologist,* vol. 56, pp. 973–1002.

BARRINGER, HERBERT R.; BLANKSTEN, GEORGE I.; and MACK, RAYMOND W. (Eds.).

1965   *Social Change in Developing Areas: A Reinterpretation of Evolutionary Theory.* Cambridge, Mass.. (Schenkman Pub. Co.).

BATES, MARSTON

1952   *Where Winter Never Comes; A Study of Man and Nature in the Tropics.* New York (Scribner).

BAUDIN, LOUIS

1961   *A Socialist Empire: The Incas of Peru.* Princeton (Van Nostrand).

BEALS, RALPH
1953   See Kroeber, Alfred L. (Ed.).

BEAUVOIR, SIMONE DE
1953   *The Second Sex.* New York (Knopf).

BELL, DANIEL
1960   *The End of Ideology: On the Exhaustion of Political Ideas in the Fifties.* Glencoe, Ill. (Free Press).
1964   See Ginzberg, Eli (Ed.).

BENEDICT, RUTH
1934   *Patterns of Culture.* New York (Houghton Mifflin).

BENNETT, WENDELL C.
1964   "The Archeology of the Central Andes." *Handbook of South American Indians,* Bureau of American Ethnology, Bull. 143, vol. 2, pp. 61–147. Washington, D.C.

BENNETT, WENDELL C., and BIRD, JUNIUS
1949   *Andean Culture History.* New York (American Museum of Natural History).

BENTANCOURT DIAS, JESÚS
1961   *La Filosofía de la Historia de Arnold J. Toynbee.* Montevideo.

BERDAIEFF, NIKOLAI A.
1962   *The Meaning of History.* Cleveland (Meridian Books).

BERLE, JR., ADOLF A., and MEANS, GARDINER C.
1937   *The Modern Corporation and Private Property.* New York (Macmillan).

BERLINER, J. S.
1962   "The Feet of the Native are Large: An Essay on Anthropology by an Economist." *Current Anthropology,* vol. 3, pp. 47–77.

BERNAL, IGNACIO

1953 *Mesoamérica: Período Indígena.* Mexico (Instituto Panamericano de Geografía e Historia).

BERNAL, JOHN D.

1954 *Science in History.* London (Watts).
1958 *World Without War.* London (Routledge and Paul).

BLOCH, MARC L. B.

1961 *Feudal Society.* Chicago (Univ. of Chicago Press).

BOSCH-GIMPERA, PEDRO

1960 *El Problema Indoeuropeo.* Mexico (Universidad Nacional Autónoma).

BRAIDWOOD, ROBERT J.

1952 *The Near East and the Foundations for Civilization.* Eugene (Oregon State System of Higher Education).
1957 *Prehistoric Men.* Chicago (Field Museum).

BRIGGS, A., and others

1963 *Technology and Economic Development.* New York.

BRIÚSOV, A.; SÁJAROV, A.; FADEIEV, A.; CHERMENSKI, E.; and SÓLIKOV, G.

n.d. *Historia de la URSS.* Moscow (Ediciones en Lenguas Extrangeras).

BURCKHARDT, JAKOB C.

1929 *The Civilization of the Renaissance in Italy.* London (G. G. Harrap and Co., Ltd.).

CARR, EDWARD HALLETT

1951 *The New Society.* London (Macmillan).

CASO, ALFONSO

1958 *The Aztecs: People of the Sun.* Norman (Univ. of Oklahoma Press).

CASTRO, JOSUÉ DE

1952　*The Geography of Hunger.* Boston (Little, Brown).

CÈPÉDE, M.; HOUTART, F.; and GROND, L.

1964　*Population and Food.* New York (Sheed and Ward).
1967　*La Población Mundial y los Medios de Subsistencia.* Barcelona (Editorial Nova Terra).

CHAND, TARA

1944　*A Short History of the Indian People from the Earliest Times to the Present Day.* Calcutta (Macmillan).

CHESNEAUX, J.

1964　"Le Mode de Production Asiatique: Quelques Perspectives de Recherche." *La Pensée,* no. 114. Paris.

CHESNOKOV, D. I.

1966　*Materialismo Histórico.* Montevideo (Ediciones Pueblos Unidos).

CHILDE, V. GORDON

1934　*New Light on the Most Ancient East.* London (K. Paul, Trench, Truber and Co.).
1936　*Man Makes Himself.* London (Watts and Co.).
1944a　"Archaeological Ages as Technological Stages." *Journal of the Royal Anthropological Institute,* vol. 74, pp. 7–24.
1944b　*Progress and Archaeology.* London (Watts and Co.).
1946　*What Happened in History.* New York (Penguin Books).
1951　*Social Evolution.* London (Watts).
1954　See Singer, Charles J., and others (Eds.).
1956　*Society and Knowledge.* New York (Harper).

CIPOLLA, CARLO M.

1962　*The Economic History of World Population.* Baltimore (Penguin Books).

CLAIRMONTE, FRÉDÉRIC

1960　*Economic Liberalism and Underdevelopment: Studies in the Disintegration of an Idea.* London (Asia Pub. House).

CLARK, COLIN
1957   *The Conditions of Economic Progress.* London (Macmillan).

COMTE, AUGUSTE
1840   *Cours de Philosophie Positive,* vol. 4. Paris (Bachelier).

CONDORCET, MARIE JEAN ANTOINE NICOLAS CARITAT
1955   *Sketch for a Historical Picture of the Progress of the Human Mind.*
       London (Weidenfeld and Nicolson).

CONKLIN, HAROLD C.
1961   "The Study of Shifting Cultivation." *Current Anthropology,* vol. 2,
       pp. 27–61.

CORTESÁO, JAIME
1947   *Los Portugueses: Historia de América y de los Pueblos Americanos,*
       vol. 3. Barcelona (Salvat).

COTTRELL, WILLIAM FREDERICK
1955   *Energy and Society: The Relation Between Energy, Social Change, and
       Economic Development.* New York (McGraw Hill).

COULBORN, RUSHTON (Ed.).
1956   *Feudalism in History.* Princeton (Princeton Univ. Press).

CREEL, HERRLEE G.
1937   *Studies in Early Chinese Culture.* Baltimore (Waverly Press).

CROUZET, MAURICE
1957   "L'Époque Contemporaine, à la Recherche d'une Civilisation Nou-
       velle." *Histoire Générale des Civilisations,* vol. 7. Paris (Presses Uni-
       versitaires de France).

CUNNINGHAM, WILLIAM
1911   *An Essay on Western Civilization and Its Economic Aspects.* Cam-
       bridge (University Press).

CUNOW, HEINRICH

1933 *La Organización Social del Imperio de los Incas, Investigación Sobre el Comunismo Agrario en el Antiguo Perú.* Lima (Libraría y Editorial Peruana de D. Miranda).

CURWEN, ELIOT C., and HATT, GUDMUND

1953 *Plough and Pasture, the Early History of Farming.* New York (H. Schuman).

DAHRENDORFF, RALF

1959 *Class and Class Conflict in Industrial Society.* Stanford (Stanford Univ. Press).

DAVIS, KINGSLEY

1955 "The Origin and Growth of the Urbanization in the World." *American Journal of Sociology,* vol. 60, pp. 428–437.

DAVIS, KINGSLEY (Ed.).

1945 *World Population in Transition.* Philadelphia (American Acad. of Pol. and Soc. Science, Annals, vol. 237).

DE CARLO, CHARLES R.

1964 See Ginzberg, Eli (Ed.).

DEL BARCO, OSCAR

1965 "Las Formaciones Económicas Precapitalistas de Karl Marx." *Pasado y Presente,* vol. 9, pp. 84–96. Córdoba, Argentina.

DIAMOND, STANLEY (Ed.).

1960 *Culture in History, Essays in Honor of Paul Radin.* New York (Columbia Univ. Press).

DITTMER, KUNZ

1953 *Allgemeine Völkerkunde: Formen und Entwicklung der Kultur.* Braunschweig (F. Vieweg).

DJILAS, MILOVAN

1957 *The New Class: An Analysis of the Communist System.* New York (Praeger).

DOBB, MAURICE H.

1925 *Capitalist Enterprise and Social Progress.* London (G. Routledge and Sons).
1948 *Soviet Economic Development Since 1917.* London (Routledge and K. Paul).
1964 *Studies in the Development of Capitalism.* New York (International Publishers).

DOBYNS, H. F. and THOMPSON, PAUL

1966 "Estimating Aboriginal American Population." *Current Anthropology,* vol. 7, pp. 395–449.

DOLE, GERTRUDE E., and CARNEIRO, ROBERT L. (Eds.).

1960 *Essays in the Science of Culture.* New York (Thomas Y. Crowell).

DORSELAER, JAIME, and GREGORY, ALFONSO

1962 *La Urbanización en América Latina.* Bogotá (Centro Internacional de Investigaciones Sociales de FERES).

DRIOTON, ETIENNE, and VANDIER, J.

1952 *L'Egypt.* Paris.

DUMAS, MAURICE (Ed.).

1963 *Histoire Générale des Techniques.* Paris.

DUMONT, RENÉ

1957 *Types of Rural Economy: Studies in World Agriculture.* New York (Praeger).

DURKHEIM, EMILE

1964 *The Division of Labor in Society.* New York (Free Press of Glencoe).
1965 *The Elementary Forms of the Religious Life.* New York (Free Press).

EISENSTADT, SHMUEL N.

1963a *Modernization: Growth and Diversity.* Bloomington (Dept. of Govt., Indiana Univ.).
1963b *The Political Systems of Empires.* New York (Free Press of Glencoe).
1964   "Social Change: Differentiation and Evolution." *American Sociological Review,* vol. 29, pp. 375–386.

ENGELS, FRIEDRICH

1942   *The Origin of the Family, Private Property and the State, in the Light of the Researches of Lewis H. Morgan.* New York (International Publishers).
1949   *The Part Played by Labour in the Transition from Ape to Man.* Moscow (Foreign Languages Pub. House).
1950   *The Condition of the Working-Class in England in 1844.* London (G. Allen and Unwin).
1964   *Dialectics of Nature.* 3rd rev. ed. Moscow (Progress Publishers).

FANON, FRANTZ

1965   *The Wretched of the Earth.* New York (Grove Press).

FERGUSON, WILLIAM S.

1913   *Greek Imperialism.* Boston and New York (Houghton Mifflin).

FLEMING, ARTHUR P. M., and BROCKLEHURST, H. J.

1925   *A History of Engineering.* London (A. and C. Black Ltd.).

FORD, C. DARRYL

1949   *Habitat, Economy and Society.* London (Methuen).

FOSTER, GEORGE M.

1960   *Culture and Conquest: America's Spanish Heritage.* New York (Wenner-Gren Foundation).
1962   *Traditional Cultures and the Impact of Technological Change.* New York (Harper).
1965   "Peasant Society and the Image of Limited Good." *American Anthropologist,* vol. 67, pp. 293–315.

FOURASTIÉ, JEAN

1949   *Le Grand Espoir du XX Siècle.* Paris (Presses Universitaires de France).
1960   *The Causes of Wealth.* Glencoe, Ill. (Free Press).

FRANK, ANDREW GUNDER

1967a *Capitalism and Underdevelopment in Latin America: Historical Studies of Chile and Brazil.* New York (Monthly Review Press).
1967b "Sociology of Development and Underdevelopment of Sociology." *Catalyst,* no. 3, pp. 20–73. Buffalo.

FRANTSOV, G. P.

1966 *El Pensamiento Social: Su Trayectoria Histórica.* Montevideo (Ediciones Pueblos Unidos).

FRIED, MORTON H.

1960 See Diamond, Stanley (Ed.).
1967 *The Evolution of Political Society: An Essay in Political Anthropology.* New York (Random House).

FROMM, ERICH

1955 *The Sane Society.* New York (Rinehart).

FURTADO, CELSO

1966 *Subdesenvolvimento e Estagnação na América Latina.* Rio de Janeiro (Civilização Brasileira).

GALBRAITH, JOHN K.

1958 *The Affluent Society.* Boston (Houghton Mifflin).

GANNAGÉ, ELIAS A.

1962 *Economie du Développement.* Paris (Presses Universitaires de France).

GARCÍA, ANTONIO

1948 "Regímenes Indígenas de Salario: El Salario Natural y el Salario Capitalista en la Historia de América." *América Indígena,* vol. 8, no. 4. Mexico.

GARDET, LOUIS

1954 *La Cité Musulmane: Vie Sociale et Politique.* Paris (J. Vrin).

GENNEP, ARNOLD VAN

1922 "Traité Comparatif des Nationalités." *Les Éléments Extérieurs de la Nationalité*, vol. 1. Paris (Payot and Cie).

GERSCHENKRON, ALEXANDER

1962 *Economic Backwardness in Historical Perspective.* Cambridge (Belknap Press of Harvard Univ. Press).

GINZBERG, ELI (Ed.)

1964 *Technology and Social Change.* New York (Columbia Univ. Press).

GLOTZ, GUSTAVE

1965 *The Greek City and Its Institutions.* New York (Barnes and Noble).

GLUCKMAN, MAX, and EGGAN, FRED

1965 *Introduction: Political Systems and the Distribution of Power. A.S.A. Monographs,* No. 2. London.

GODELIER, MAURICE

1964 *La Notion de "Mode de Production Asiatique" et les Schémas Marxistes d'Évolution des Sociétés.* Paris (Centre d'Études et de Recherches Marxistes).

GOUROU, PIERRE

1953 *The Tropical World, Its Social and Economic Conditions and Its Future Status.* London, New York (Longmans, Green).

GRAEBNER, FRITZ

1924 *Das Weltbild der Primitiven.* Munich (E. Reinhardt).

GREKOV, BORIS D.

1947 *The Culture of Kiev Rūs.* Moscow (Foreign Languages Pub. House).

GROUSSET, RENÉ

1939 *L'Empire des Steppes: Attila, Gengis Khan, Tamerlan.* Paris (Payot).
1944 *Les Croisades.* Paris (Presses Universitaires de France).

GUENTHER, R.; SCHROT, G., and others

1960   *Estado y Classes en la Antiguedad Esclavista.* Buenos Aires (Editorial Platina).

GUMPLOWICZ, LUDWIG

1883   *Der Rassenkampf.* Innsbruck (Wagner'sche Univ.-Buchhandlung).

HAGEN, EVERETT E.

1962   *On the Theory of Social Change: How Economic Growth Begins* Homewood, Ill. (Dorsey Press).

HALPERIN, MORTON H.

1965   *China and the Bomb.* New York (Praeger).
1967   *Contemporary Military Strategy.* Boston (Little, Brown).

HARDOY, JORGE E.

1964   *Ciudades Precolombinas.* Buenos Aires (Ediciones Infinito).

HARING, CLARENCE H.

1947   *The Spanish Empire in America.* New York (Oxford Univ. Press).

HAWKES, JACQUETTA

1963   *Prehistory. History of Mankind, Cultural and Scientific Development,* vol. 1, part 1. (UNESCO).

HEGEL, G. W. F.

1881   *Lectures on the Philosophy of History.* London (G. Bell and Sons).

HEISER, CHARLES B.

1965   "Cultivated Plants and Cultural Diffusion in Nuclear America." *American Anthropologist,* vol. 67, pp. 930–949.

HENRY, JULES

1963   *Culture Against Man.* New York (Random House).

HERSKOVITS, MELVILLE J.

1938 *Acculturation: The Study of Culture Contact.* New York (J. J. Augustin).
1952 *Economic Anthropology.* New York (Knopf).

HIRSHMAN, A. D.

1945 *National Power and the Structure of Foreign Trade.* Berkeley.

HOBSBAWM, ERIC J.

1965 "Introduction." See Marx, Karl.

HOBSON, JOHN A.

1965 *Imperialism, a Study.* Ann Arbor (Univ. of Michigan Press).

HOCKETT, CHARLES F., and ASCHER, ROBERT

1964 "The Human Revolution." *Current Anthropology,* vol. 5, pp. 135–147.

HODGMAN, DONALD R., and BERGSON, A. (Eds.).

1954 *Soviet Economic Growth.* New York.

HOEBEL, E. ADAMSON

1954 *The Law of Primitive Man.* Cambridge (Harvard Univ. Press).

HOLTON, GERALD J. (Ed.).

1965 *Science and Culture, a Study of Cohesive and Disjunctive Forces.* Boston (Houghton Mifflin).

HOROWITZ, IRVING LOUIS

1966 *Three Worlds of Development: The Theory and Practice of International Stratification.* New York (Oxford Univ. Press).

HOSELITZ, BERT F.

1953 "The Role of Cities in the Economic Growth of Underdeveloped Countries." *Journal of Political Economy,* vol. 51, pp. 195–208.
1960 *Sociological Aspects of Economic Growth.* Glencoe, Ill. (Free Press).

HUIZINGA, JOHAN
1924   *The Waning of the Middle Ages.* London (E. Arnold and Co.).

HUNTER, MONICA
1956   *Reaction to Conquest.* London, New York (Oxford Univ. Press).

HUNTINGTON, ELLSWORTH
1927   *The Human Habitat.* New York (D. Van Nostrand Co.).

HUXLEY, JULIAN S.
1955   "Evolution, Cultural and Biological." *Yearbook of Anthropology,* pp. 3–25. New York (Wenner-Gren Foundation).

IMBELLONI, JOSÉ
1953   *Epítome de Culturología.* Buenos Aires (Editorial Nova).

JALÉE, PIERRE
1968   *The Pillage of the Third World.* New York (Monthly Review Press).

JASPERS, KARL
1953   *The Origin and Goal of History.* New Haven (Yale Univ. Press).

JOHNSON, E. D.
1964   See Ginzberg, Eli (Ed.).

KAHN, HERMAN
1962   *Thinking About the Unthinkable.* New York (Horizon Press).

KAROL, K. S.
1967   *China: The Other Communism.* New York (Hill and Wang).

KAUTSKY, KARL
1925   *The Economic Doctrines of Karl Marx.* London (A. and C. Black).

KLEIN, JULIUS

1964 *The Mesta: A Study in Spanish Economic History, 1273–1836.* Port Washington, N.Y. (Kennikat Press).

KLUCKHOHN, CLYDE

1953 See Kroeber, Alfred L. (Ed.).

KOHN, HANS

1945 *The Idea of Nationalism: A Study of Its Origins and Background.* New York (Macmillan).

KON, I.; CHAQUIN, B.; and others

1962 *El Desarrollo en la Naturaleza y en la Sociedad.* Buenos Aires (Editorial Platina).

KOVALIEV, SERGUEI I.

1960 See Guenther, R.; Schrot, G.; and others.

KRADER, LAWRENCE

1968 *Formation of the State.* Englewood Cliffs, N.J. (Prentice-Hall).

KROEBER, ALFRED L.

1939 *Cultural and Natural Areas of Native North America.* Berkeley (Univ. of California Press).
1944 *Configurations of Cultural Growth.* Berkeley (Univ. of California Press).
1946 "The Chibcha." *Handbook of South American Indians,* Bureau of American Ethnology, Bull. 143, vol. 2, pp. 887–909. Washington.
1948 *Anthropology.* New York (Harcourt, Brace).
1952 "Toynbee's 'A Study of History.'" *The Nature of Culture,* pp. 373–378. Chicago (Univ. of Chicago Press).
1962 *A Roster of Civilizations and Culture.* Chicago (Aldine).

KROEBER, ALFRED L. (Ed.).

1953 *Anthropology Today: An Encyclopedic Inventory.* Chicago (Univ. of Chicago Press).

KROPOTKIN, PETR A.

1955 *Mutual Aid; A Factor of Evolution.* Boston (Extending Horizons Books).

KUO, MO JO

1960 See Guenther, R.; Schrot, G.; and others.

KUUSINEN, OTTO V., and others

1963 *Fundamentals of Marxism-Leninism, Manual.* Moscow (Foreign Languages Pub. House).

KUZNETS, SIMON S.

1946 *National Income; A Survey of Findings.* New York (Nat. Bur. of Economic Research).
1964 *Postwar Economic Growth, Four Lectures.* Cambridge, Mass. (Belknap Press of Harvard University).

LACOSTE, YVES

1959 *Les Pays Sous-développés.* Paris (Presses Universitaires de France).
n.d.   *Introducción Bibliográfica al Desarrollo Económico y Social.* Montevideo.

LANDRY, ADOLPHE

1949 *Traité de Démographie.* Paris (Payot).

LANGE, OSCAR R.

1963 *General Problems. Political Economy,* vol. 1. Oxford, New York (Pergamon Press).
1966 *La Economía en las Sociedades Modernas.* Mexico (Editorial Grijaldo).

LASKI, HAROLD J.

1943 *Reflections on the Revolution of Our Time.* New York (Viking).

LATTIMORE, OWEN

1940 *Inner Asian Frontiers of China.* London, New York (Oxford Univ. Press).

LAVIOSA ZAMBOTTI, PIA

1958 *Origen y Difusión de la Civilización.* Barcelona (Omega).
1959 *Origen y Destino de la Cultura Occidental.* Madrid (Ediciones Guadarrama).

LEA, HENRY CHARLES

1908 *The Inquisition in the Spanish Dependencies.* New York (Macmillan).

LEBRET, LOUIS JOSEPH

1959 *Manifeste pour une Civilisation Solidaire.* Caluire (Économie et Humanisme).

LENIN, VLADEMIR I.

1947 *The State and Revolution.* Moscow (Foreign Languages Pub. House).
1951 *Imperialism, the Highest Stage of Capitalism.* Moscow (Foreign Languages Pub. House).
1956 *The Development of Capitalism in Russia.* Moscow (Foreign Languages Pub. House).

LERNER, DANIEL

1958 *The Passing of Traditional Society: Modernizing the Middle East.* Glencoe, Ill. (Free Press).

LERNER, DANIEL, and LASSWELL, HAROLD D. (Eds.).

1965 *The Policy Sciences.* Stanford (Stanford Univ. Press).

LEROI-GOURHAN, ANDRÉ

1943 *L'Homme et la Matière.* Paris (A. Michel).
1945 *Milieu et Techniques.* Paris (A. Michel).
1963 See Dumas, Maurice (Ed.).

LEVI-STRAUSS, CLAUDE
1949 *Les Structures Élémentaires de la Parenté.* Paris (Presses Universitaires de France).
1953 See Kroeber, Alfred L. (Ed.).

LEVY, REUBEN

1957 *The Social Structure of Islam.* Cambridge (University Press).

LEWIN, BOLESLAO

1962   *La Inquisición en Hispanoamérica.* Buenos Aires (Editorial Proyección).

LILLEY, SAMUEL

1948   *Men, Machines and History.* London (Cobbett Press).

LINTON, RALPH

1936   *The Study of Man.* New York (D. Appleton-Century).
1955   *The Tree of Culture.* New York (Knopf).

LINTON, RALPH (Ed.).

1945   *The Science of Man in the World Crisis.* New York (Columbia Univ. Press).

LIST, FRIEDERICH

1966   *The National System of Political Economy.* New York (A. M. Kelley).

LOWIE, ROBERT H.

1927   *The Origin of the State.* New York (Harcourt, Brace).

LUXEMBURG, ROSA

1951   *The Accumulation of Capital.* New Haven (Yale Univ. Press).

MACIVER, ROBERT M.

1942   *Social Causation.* Boston (Ginn and Co.).

MAHAN, ALFRED THAYER

1890   *The Influence of Sea Power Upon History, 1660–1783.* Boston (Little, Brown and Co.).

MAKAROV, A. (Ed.).

1965   *Manual de Materialismo Histórico.* Buenos Aires (Editorial Cartago).

MALINOWSKI, BRONISLAW

1944 *A Scientific Theory of Culture.* Chapel Hill (Univ. of North Carolina Press).
1945 *The Dynamics of Culture Change.* New Haven (Yale Univ. Press).

MANNHEIM, KARL

1936 *Ideology and Utopia.* New York (Harcourt, Brace).
1944 *Diagnosis of Our Time.* New York (Oxford Univ. Press).
1950 *Freedom, Power and Democratic Planning.* New York (Oxford Univ. Press).

MAO, TSÊ-TUNG

1966 *Cuatro Tesis Filosóficas.* Peking.

MARIÁTEGUI, JOSÉ CARLOS

1955 *Siete Ensayos de Interpretación de la Realidad Peruana.* Santiago de Chile (Editorial Universitaria).

MARTÍNEZ DEL RÍO, PABLO

1943 *Los Orígenes Americanos.* Mexico.

MARX, KARL

1904 *A Contribution to the Critique of Political Economy.* New York (International Library Pub. Co.).
1965 *Pre-Capitalist Economic Formations.* New York (International Publishers).
1967 *Capital: A Critique of Political Economy.* New York (International Publishers).

MARX, KARL, and ENGELS, FRIEDRICH

1934 *Correspondence, 1846–1895.* London (M. Lawrence Ltd.).
1958 *La Ideología Alemana.* Montevideo.
1964 *Sobre el Sistema Colonial del Capitalismo.* Buenos Aires. (Ediciones Estudio).

MASPÉRO, GEORGES

1929–1930 *Un Empire Colonial Français, l'Indochine.* Paris (Éditions G. Van Oest).

MASSÉ, HENRI (Ed.).
1952   *La Civilization Iranienne.* Paris.

MAURO, FRÉDÉRIC
1964   *L'Expansion Européenne 1600–1870.* Paris (Presses Universitaires de France).

McINNIS, EDGAR, and others
1951   *Ensayos Sobre la Historia del Nuevo Mundo.* Mexico (Pan American Institute of Geography and History).

MEAD, MARGARET
1966   *Continuities in Cultural Evolution.* New Haven (Yale Univ. Press).

MEAD, MARGARET (Ed.).
1953   *Cultural Patterns and Technical Change.* Paris (UNESCO).

MEGGERS, BETTY J.
1960   See Dole, Gertrude E., and Carneiro, Robert L. (Eds.).
ms.   "Prehistoric New World Cultural Development." *History of Mankind, Cultural and Scientific Development,* vol. 3. (UNESCO). In press.

MEGGERS, BETTY J. (Ed.).
1956   "Functional and Evolutionary Implications of Community Patterning." *Society for American Archaeology Memoir 11,* pp. 129–157.
1959   *Evolution and Anthropology: A Centennial Appraisal.* Washington (Anthropological Society of Washington).

MEGGERS, BETTY J., and EVANS, CLIFFORD (Eds.).
1963   *Aboriginal Cultural Development in Latin America; An Interpretative Review.* Washington (Smithsonian Institution).

MENDÈS-FRANCE, PIERRE, and ARDANT, GABRIEL
1955   *Economics and Action.* New York (Columbia Univ. Press).

MERTON, ROBERT K.
1957   *Social Theory and Social Structure.* Glencoe, Ill. (Free Press).

METCHNIKOV, LEV ILITCH

1889   *La Civilisation et les Grandes Fleuves Historiques.* Paris.

MILLS, CHARLES WRIGHT

1956   *The Power Elite.* New York (Oxford Univ. Press).
1958   *The Causes of World War Three.* New York (Simon and Schuster).

MONTAGU, ASHLEY M. F.

1955   *The Direction of Human Development.* New York (Harper).
1965   *The Human Revolution.* Cleveland (World Publishing Co.).

MONTANDON, GEORGE

1934   *L'Ologénèse Culturelle. Traité d'Ethnologie Cyclo-culturelle et d'Ergologie Systématique.* Paris (Payot).

MORGAN, LEWIS HENRY

1870   *Systems of Consanguinity and Affinity of the Human Family.* Washington (Smithsonian Institution).
1877   *Ancient Society.* New York (H. Holt and Co.).

MORLEY, SYLVANUS G.

1946   *The Ancient Maya.* Stanford (Stanford Univ. Press).

MOUSSA, PIERRE

1959   *Les Nations Prolétaires.* Paris (Presses Universitaires de France).

MÜLLER-LYER, F.

1930   *La Familia.* Madrid.

MUMFORD, LEWIS

1938   *The Culture of Cities.* New York (Harcourt, Brace).
1961   *The City in History: Its Origins, Its Transformations and Its Prospects.* New York (Harcourt, Brace and World).
1963   *Technics and Civilization.* New York (Harcourt, Brace and World).

MURDOCK, GEORGE P.

1947 See Linton, Ralph (Ed.).
1949 *Social Structure.* New York (Macmillan).
1951 *Outline of South American Cultures.* New Haven (Human Relations Area Files).

MYRDAL, GUNNAR

1957 *Economic Theory and Under-developed Regions.* London (G. Duckworth).
1961 *El Estado del Futuro.* Mexico.

NAQUET, PIERRE VIDAL

1964 *Histoire et Idéologie: Karl Wittfogel et le Concept de "Modes de Production Asiatique."* Annales: Economies, Sociétés, Civilizations, vol. 19, Paris.

NAROLL, RAOUL

1964 "On Ethnic Unit Classification." *Current Anthropology,* vol. 4, pp. 283–291.

NEF, JOHN U.

1950 *War and Human Progress: An Essay on the Rise of Industrial Civilization.* Cambridge (Harvard Univ. Press).
1958 *Cultural Foundations of Industrial Civilization.* Cambridge (University Press).

NKRUMAH, KWAME

1965 *Neo-Colonialism: The Last Stage of Imperialism.* London (Nelson).

NOL'DE, BORIS E.

1952–1953 *La Formation de l'Empire Russe.* Paris (Institut d'Études Slaves).

NORDENSKIOLD, ERLAND

1930 *Modifications in Indian Culture Through Inventions and Loans.* Göteborg (Comparative Ethnographical Studies No. 8).
1931 *Origin of the Indian Civilizations in South America.* Göteborg (Comparative Ethnographical Studies No. 9).

NOVIKOV, JACQUES
1902   *L'Avenir de la Race Blanche.* Paris.

OGBURN, WILLIAM F.
1926   *Social Change.* New York (B.W. Huebsch).

OKLADNIKOV, A.
1962   See Kon, I.; Chaquin, B.; and others.

OLIVEIRA MARTINS, JOAQUIM P.
1930   *A History of Iberian Civilization.* London (Oxford Univ. Press).

OPLER, MORRIS E.
1964   "Morgan and Materialism: A Reply." *Current Anthropology,* vol. 5, pp. 110–114.

OPPENHEIMER, J. ROBERT
1954   *Science and the Common Understanding.* New York (Simon and Schuster).

OSGOOD, CORNELIUS
1951   *The Koreans and Their Culture.* New York (Ronald Press).

OTS CAPDEQUI, JOSÉ MARÍA
1946   *El Estado Español de las Indias.* Mexico (Fondo de Cultura Económica).

OWEN, ROGER C.
1965   "The Patrilocal Band: A Linguistically and Culturally Hybrid Unit." *American Anthropologist,* vol. 67, pp. 675–690.

PALERM, ANGEL
1955   See Steward, Julian H. (Ed.).

PALERM, ANGEL, and WOLF, ERIC

1961   "La Agricultura y el Desarrollo de la Civilización en Mesoamérica." *Revista Interamericana de Ciencias Sociales,* vol. 1, no. 2. Washington (Pan American Union).

PALLOTTINO, MASSIMO

1955   *The Etruscans.* Harmondsworth (Penguin Books).

PARRY, JOHN H.

1949   *Europe and a Wider World, 1415–1715.* London, New York (Hutchinson's University Library).

PARSONS, TALCOTT

1964   "Evolutionary Universals in Society." *American Sociological Review,* vol. 29, pp. 339–357.

PASDERMADJIAN, H.

1960   *La Segunda Revolución Industrial.* Madrid. (Editorial Tecnos).

PERICOT GARCÍA, LUIS

1962   *América Indígena.* Barcelona (Salvat Editores).

PERROUX, FRANÇOIS

1958   *La Coexistence Pacifique.* Paris (Presses Universitaires de France).
1961   *L'Économie du XXe Siècle.* Paris (Presses Universitaires de France).

PIETTRE, ANDRÉ

1955   *Les Trois Âges de l'Économie.* Paris (Éditions Ouvrières).

PIGGOTT, STUART

1950   *Prehistoric India.* Harmondsworth (Penguin Books).

PINTO, LUIZ DE AGUIAR COSTA

1967   *Desenvolvimento Econômico e Transição Social.* Rio de Janeiro (Univ. Federal do Rio de Janeiro).

PIRENNE, HENRI

1937   *Economic and Social History of Medieval Europe.* New York (Harcourt, Brace).

PIRENNE, JACQUES

1962   *The Tides of History.* New York (Dutton).

PLEKHANOV, G. V.

1940   *The Role of the Individual in History.* New York (International Publishers).
1947   *In Defence of Materialism: The Development of the Monist View of History.* London (Lawrence and Wishart).

PONOMAREV, BORIS N., and others

1962   *History of the Communist Party of the Soviet Union.* Moscow (Foreign Languages Pub. House).

PRICE, DON K.

1965   See Holton, Gerald J. (Ed.).

QUINTERO, RODOLFO

1964   *Antropología de las Ciudades Latinoamericanas.* Caracas (Universidad Central de Venezuela).

RADCLIFFE-BROWN, A. R.

1931   *The Present Position of Anthropological Studies.* London (British Assoc. for the Adv. of Science).
1940   "Preface," to Fortes, M., and Evans-Pritchard, E. E. (Eds.), *African Political Systems.* Oxford (Oxford Univ. Press).

REDFIELD, ROBERT

1953   *The Primitive World and its Transformations.* Ithaca (Cornell Univ. Press).
1956   *Peasant Society and Culture.* Chicago (Univ. of Chicago Press).

REDFIELD, ROBERT, and SINGER, M. B.

1954   "The Cultural Role of Cities." *Economic Development and Cultural Change,* vol. 3, pp. 53–74.

REDFIELD, ROBERT; LINTON, RALPH; and HERSKOVITS, M. J.

1936   "Memorandum for the Study of Acculturation." *American Anthropologist*, vol. 38, pp. 149–152.

RENOUVIN, PIERRE

1949   "Introduction." *Les Politiques d'Expansion Imperialiste.* Paris.

REVELLE, ROGER

1963   See Briggs, A., and others.

ROMERO, JOSÉ LUIS

1967   *La Revolución Burguesa en el Mundo Feudal.* Buenos Aires (Editorial Sudamericana).

ROSTOVTSEV, MIKHAIL I.

1926   *The Social and Economic History of the Roman Empire.* Oxford (Clarendon Press).

ROSTOW, WALT W.

1960   *The Process of Economic Growth.* New York (Norton).
1964   *The Stages of Economic Growth: A Non-Communist Manifesto.* Cambridge (University Press).

ROUSE, IRVING

1953   See Kroeber, Alfred L. (Ed.).

RUMIANTSEV, ALEXEI M. (Ed.).

1963   *Structure of the Working Class.* New Delhi (People's Pub. House).

SAHLINS, MARSHALL D.

1968   *Tribesmen.* Englewood Cliffs (Prentice-Hall).

SAHLINS, MARSHALL D., and SERVICE, ELMAN R. (Eds.).

1960   *Evolution and Culture.* Ann Arbor (Univ. of Michigan Press).

SÁNCHEZ-ALBORÑOZ, C.

1946 *La España Musulmana.* Buenos Aires (El Ateneo).
1956 *España, Un Enigma Histórico.* Buenos Aires (Editorial Sudamericana).

SAPIR, EDWARD

1924 "Culture, Genuine and Spurious." *American Journal of Sociology,* vol. 29, pp. 401–429.

SAUER, CARL O.

1952 *Agricultural Origins and Dispersals.* New York (American Geographical Society).

SAUVY, ALFRED

1952–1954 *Théorie Générale de la Population.* Paris (Presses Universitaires de France).
1961 *Fertility and Survival: Population Problems from Malthus to Mao Tse-Tung.* New York (Criterion Books).

SAYCE, RODERICK U.

1965 *Primitive Arts and Crafts.* New York (Bilbo and Tannen).

SCHEMELIOV, N. P.

1965 *Los Ideólogos del Imperialismo y los Problemas de los Países Sub-desarrollados.* Bogotá (Ediciones Suramerica Ltda.).

SCHMIDT, MAX

1926 *The Primitive Races of Mankind: A Study in Ethnology.* London (G. G. Harrap).

SCHMIDT, W., and KOPPERS, W.

1924 *Völker und Kulturen.* Regensburg.

SCHRECKER, PAUL

1948 *Work and History: An Essay on the Structure of Civilization.* Princeton (Princeton Univ. Press).

SCHUMPETER, JOSEPH A.
1951 *Imperialism and Social Classes.* New York (A. M. Kelley).
1956 *Capitalism, Socialism and Democracy.* New York (Harper).

SÉDILLOT, RENÉ
1938 *Histoire des Colonisations.* Paris (A. Fayard).

SÉE, HENRI E.
1928 *Modern Capitalism: Its Origin and Evolution.* London (N. Douglas).

SELIGMAN, EDWIN R. A.
1961 *The Economic Interpretation of History.* New York (Columbia Univ. Press).

SERGIO, ANTONIO
1929 *Historia de Portugal.* Barcelona (Editorial Labor).

SERVICE, ELMAN R.
1962 *Primitive Social Organization: An Evolutionary Perspective.* New York (Random House).

SHTAERMAN, ELENA M.
1960 See Guenther, R.; Schrot, G.; and others.

SILVERT, KALMAN H. (Ed.).
1963 *Expectant Peoples: Nationalism and Development.* New York (Random House).

SIMPSON, GEORGE GAYLORD
1951 *The Meaning of Evolution.* New York (New American Library).

SINGER, CHARLES J. and others (Eds.).
1954–1958 *A History of Technology.* 5 vols. Oxford (Clarendon Press).

SIREAU, ALBERT
1966 *Teoría de la Población: Ecología Urbana y su Aplicación a la Argentina.* Buenos Aires (Editorial Sudamericana).

SJOBERG, GIDEON

1966   *The Pre-industrial City: Past and Present.* New York (The Free Press-Macmillan).

SNOW, CHARLES P.

1959   *The Two Cultures and the Scientific Revolution.* Cambridge (Cambridge Univ. Press).

SOBOLIEV, P.; GUIMPELSON, E.; TRUKAN, G.; and CHEBAEVSKI, F.

n.d.   *La Historia de la Gran Revolución Socialista de Octubre.* Moscow (Ed. Progreso).

SOLOVEV, VLADIMIR S.

1948   *Russia and the Universal Church.* London (G. Bles).

SOMBART, WERNER

1964   *The Quintessence of Capitalism.* New York (H. Fertig).

SOROKIN, PITRIM A.

1937–1941   *Social and Cultural Dynamics.* New York (American Book Co.).
1950   *Social Philosophies of an Age of Crisis.* Boston (Beacon Press).

SOUSTELLE, JACQUES

1961   *The Daily Life of the Aztecs.* New York (Macmillan).

SOUTHALL, AIDAN

1965   "A Critique of the Typology of States and Political Systems." *Political Systems and the Distribution of Power,* A.S.A. Monographs no. 2. London (Tavistock Publications).

SPENCER, HERBERT

1895–1897   *Principles of Sociology.* New York (D. Appleton and Co.).

SPENGLER, OSWALD

1962   *The Decline of the West.* New York (Knopf).

STALIN, JOSEPH

1940a *Marxism and the National and Colonial Question.* Moscow (Foreign Languages Pub. House).
1940b *Problems of Leninism.* Moscow (Foreign Languages Pub. House).

STAVENHAGEN, RODOLFO

1965   "Siete Tesis Equivocadas Sobre América Latina." *Política Exterior Independente,* no. 1. Rio de Janeiro.

STERN, BERNHARD J.

1931   *Lewis Henry Morgan, Social Evolutionist.* Chicago (Univ. of Chicago Press).
1946   "L. H. Morgan Today." *Science and Society,* vol. 10, pp. 172–176.
1948   "Engels on the Family." *Science and Society,* vol. 12, pp. 42–64.

STERNBERG, FRITZ

1959   *The Military and Industrial Revolution of Our Time.* New York (Praeger).

STEWARD, JULIAN H.

1950   *Area Research, Theory and Practice.* New York (Social Science Research Council).
1953   See Kroeber, Alfred L. (Ed.).
1955   *Theory of Culture Change: The Methodology of Multilinear Evolution.* Urbana (Univ. of Illinois Press).

STEWARD, JULIAN H. (Ed.).

1946–1950 *Handbook of South American Indians.* Bureau of American Ethnology, Bull. 143, vols. 1–6. Washington (Smithsonian Institution).
1955   *Irrigation Civilizations: A Comparative Study.* Washington (Pan American Union).

STEWARD, JULIAN H., and FARON, LOUIS C.

1959   *Native Peoples of South America.* New York (McGraw-Hill).

STRACHEY, JOHN

1935   *The Nature of Capitalist Crisis.* New York (Covici, Friede).
1956   *Contemporary Capitalism.* New York (Random House).
1960   *The End of Empire.* New York (Random House).

SURET-CANALE, JEAN

1958　*Afrique Noire, Occidentale et Centrale.* Paris (Éditions Sociales).

SWEEZY, PAUL M.

1942　*The Theory of Capitalist Development.* New York (Oxford Univ. Press).
1963　*Capitalismo e Imperialismo Norteamericano.* Buenos Aires.

SWEEZY, PAUL M., and others

1967　*La Transición del Feudalismo al Capitalismo.* Madrid (Editorial Ciencia Nueva).

TANNENBAUM, FRANK

1947　*Slave and Citizen: The Negro in the Americas.* New York (A. A. Knopf).

TAWNEY, RICHARD H.

1947　*Religion and the Rise of Capitalism: A Historical Study.* New York (Penguin Books).

TAX, SOL (Ed.).

1952　"The Civilizations of Ancient America." *Selected Papers of the 29th International Congress of Americanists.* Chicago (Univ. of Chicago Press).
1960　*Evolution after Darwin.* Chicago (Univ. of Chicago Press).

THURNWALD, RICHARD

1932　*Economics in Primitive Communities.* London (Oxford Univ. Press).

TOCQUEVILLE, ALEXIS DE

1960　*Democracy in America.* Introduction, editorial notes, and bibliographies by Phillips Bradley. 2 vols. New York.

TOYNBEE, ARNOLD J.

1948　*Civilization on Trial.* New York (Oxford Univ. Press).
1948–1961　*A Study of History.* London, New York (Oxford Univ. Press).
1959　*Hellenism: The History of a Civilization.* New York (Oxford Univ. Press).

TRENTIN, BRUNO

1965   *La Ideología del Neocapitalismo.* Buenos Aires.

TROTZKY, LEON

1965   *The Permanent Revolution.* New York (Pioneer Publishers).
1967   *The History of the Russian Revolution.* London (Sphere Books).

TURNER, FREDERICK J.

1962   *The Frontier in American History.* New York (Holt, Rinehart, and Winston).

TURNER, RALPH E.

1941   *The Great Cultural Traditions: The Foundations of Civilization.* New York (McGraw Hill).

TYLOR, EDWARD B.

1871   *Primitive Culture.* London (J. Murray).
1881   *Anthropology.* London (Macmillan).

UCHENKO, S. L.

1960   See Guenther, R.; Schrot, G.; and others.

UNITED NATIONS

1964a *Economic Study of Latin America, 1964.* New York (International Publications Service).
1964b *Statistical Yearbook.* New York.
1965   *Conferencia Mundial de la Población.* Boletín Informativo. New York.

USHER, ABBOTT P.

1959   *A History of Mechanical Inventions.* Boston (Beacon Press).

VAILLANT, GEORGE C.

1941   *Aztecs of Mexico.* New York (Doubleday, Doran, and Co.).

VASILIEV, ALEXANDER A.

1952   *History of the Byzantine Empire.* Madison (Univ. of Wisconsin Press).

VAVILOV, NIKOLAI I.

1926   *Studies on the Origin of Cultivated Plants.* Bull. of Applied Botany and Plant Breeding, vol. 16. Leningrad.

VEBLEN, THORSTEIN

1965   *The Theory of the Leisure Class.* New York (A. M. Kelley).

VIATKIN, A. (Ed.).

n.d.   *Compendio de Historia y Economía.* Moscow (Editorial Progreso).

VICENS VIVES, JAIME

1957–1959   *Historia Social y Económica de España y América.* Barcelona (Editorial Teide).

WASHBURN, S. L., and HOWELL, F. CLARK

1960   See Tax, Sol (Ed.).

WEBB, SIDNEY, and WEBB, BEATRICE

1936   *Soviet Communism: A New Civilization?* New York (C. Scribner's Sons).

WEBER, ALFRED

1935   *Kulturgeschichte als Kultursoziologie.* Leiden (A. W. Sijthoff).

WEBER, MAX

1947   *The Theory of Social and Economic Organization.* New York (Oxford Univ. Press).
1948   *The Protestant Ethic and the Spirit of Capitalism.* New York (Scribner).
1954   *Max Weber on Law in Economy and Society.* Cambridge (Harvard Univ. Press).

WELTFISH, GENE

1960   See Tax, Sol (Ed.).

WHEELER, MORTIMER

1953　*The Indus Civilization.* Cambridge (University Press).
1959　*Early India and Pakistan.* New York (Praeger).

WHITAKER, DOUGLAS M.

1965　See Lerner, Daniel, and Lasswell, Harold D. (Eds.).

WHITE, LESLIE A.

1945a　"History, Evolutionism and Functionalism: Three Types of Interpretation of Culture." *Southwestern Journal of Anthropology,* vol. 1, pp. 221–248.
1945b　"Diffusionism vs. Evolutionism: An Anti-evolutionist Fallacy." *American Anthropologist,* vol. 47, pp. 339–356.
1948　"Evolucionismo e Anti-evolucionismo na Teoria Etnológica Americana." *Sociologia,* vol. 10, pp. 1–39.
1949　*The Science of Culture.* New York (Farrar, Straus).
1959　*The Evolution of Culture: The Development of Civilization to the Fall of Rome.* New York (McGraw-Hill).
1960　"Foreword." See Sahlins, Marshall D., and Service, Elman R. (Eds.).

WIENER, NORBERT

1948　*Cybernetics.* New York (J. Wiley).
1950　*The Human Use of Human Beings.* Boston (Houghton Mifflin).

WILLEY, GORDON R. (Ed.).

1956　*Prehistoric Settlement Patterns in the New World.* New York (Wenner-Gren Foundation).

WILLIAMS, ERIC E.

1944　*Capitalism and Slavery.* Chapel Hill (Univ. of North Carolina Press).

WIRTH, LOUIS

1938　"Urbanism as a Way of Life." *American Journal of Sociology,* vol. 44.

WISSLER, CLARK

1938　*The American Indian: An Introduction to the Anthropology of the New World.* New York (Oxford Univ. Press).

WITTFOGEL, KARL

1955 See Steward, Julian H. (Ed.).
1957 *Oriental Despotism: A Comparative Study of Total Power.* New Haven (Yale Univ. Press).

WOLF, ERIC R.

1959 *Sons of the Shaking Earth.* Chicago (Univ. of Chicago Press).
1966 *Peasants.* Englewood Cliffs, N.J. (Prentice-Hall).

WORSLEY, PETER

1964 *The Third World.* Chicago (Univ. of Chicago Press).

ZABUROV, M. A.

1960 *Historia de las Cruzadas.* Buenos Aires.

ZIMMERMAN, L. J.

1965 *Poor Lands, Rich Lands: The Widening Gap.* New York (Random House).

ZIMMERMANN, ERICH W.

1951 *World Resources and Industries.* New York.

ZNANIECKI, FLORIAN

1944 *Las Sociedades de Cultura Nacional y sus Relaciones.* Mexico (Fondo de Cultura Económica).

Index